Moodle JavaScript Cookbook

Over 50 recipes for making your Moodle system more dynamic and responsive with JavaScript

Alastair Hole

PUBLISHING

BIRMINGHAM - MUMBAI

Moodle JavaScript Cookbook

First published: April 2011

Production Reference: 1180411

Published by Packt Publishing Ltd.
32 Lincoln Road
Olton
Birmingham, B27 6PA, UK.

ISBN 978-1-849511-90-2

www.packtpub.com

Cover Image by Rakesh Shejwal (shejwal.rakesh@gmail.com)

Credits

Author

Alastair Hole

Reviewers

Anthony Borrow

Mauno Korpelainen

Susan Smith Nash

Acquisition Editor

Chaitanya Apte

Development Editor

Roger D'souza

Technical Editor

Azharuddin Sheikh

Copy Editor

Neha Shetty

Indexer

Hemangini Bari

Editorial Team Leader

Akshara Aware

Project Team Leader

Priya Mukherji

Project Coordinator

Srimoyee Ghoshal

Proofreader

Joel T. Johnson

Production Coordinator

Kruthika Bangera

Cover Work

Kruthika Bangera

About the Author

Alastair Hole is a web software developer, who is currently specializing in educational software, particularly that which pertains to Further and Higher Education in the UK. His web development experience began in the post dot-com boom era, working on business-to-business e-commerce web applications in the publishing industry with a focus on back-office integration. He has since transferred his talents to the educational sector and has created projects which have gone on to receive awards from organizations such as The Times Educational Supplement and the IMS Global Learning Consortium.

Alastair is the author of the award-winning Moodle IMS Content Package repository plug-in "MrCUTE—Moodle Repository: Create, Upload, Tag, & Embed", which is an Open Source project commissioned by the Joint Information Systems Committee (JISC) that has seen significant use in Moodle sites worldwide, from Scotland to Australia.

Thank you to everyone who has contributed to this book's completion, be it patience with missed deadlines or encouragement when all seemed overwhelming. Thank you, Ma and Pa Hole for their foresight in recognizing that one day I would teach myself how to reassemble everything that I have ever unscrewed, detached, disassembled, or otherwise fiddled with. Thank you to The Internet for being an ever expanding well of autodidactic opportunity.

And remember, "It's just a ride. And we can change it any time we want."

About the Reviewers

Anthony Borrow, S.J. is a Jesuit of the New Orleans Province who has been active in the Moodle community for five years. Anthony has an M.A. in Counseling from Saint Louis University, and a Masters of Divinity from the Jesuit School of Theology of Santa Clara University. Anthony has worked on the design and implementation of various database systems since 1992.

Anthony serves the Moodle community as its CONTRIB Coordinator. In that role, Anthony has presented at various MoodleMoots (conferences) across the United States and provided in-house training opportunities for institutions learning how to implement Moodle. Anthony is currently the Campus Minister at Cristo Rey Jesuit College Preparatory (http://cristoreyjesuit.org/) and provides technical advice to the Jesuit Secondary Education Association (http://jsea.org) and the Jesuit Virtual Learning Academy (http://jvla.org/).

Anthony is the co-author of the Honduras chapter of Teen Gangs: A Global View, and also has been a technical reviewer of various Packt books.

> I am grateful to the Moodle community for continually inspiring me to learn more about educational technologies and fostering an environment where every voice contributes to building that community.

Mauno Korpelainen teaches Mathematics for high school and adult students in Hyvinkää, Finland, has been a PHM (Particularly Helpful Moodler) for several years, and is one of the moderators of the moodle.org forums.

Susan Smith Nash is currently the Director of Education and Professional Development for the American Association of Petroleum Geologists (AAPG) in Tulsa, Oklahoma, and an adjunct professor at The University of Oklahoma. She was the Associate Dean for graduate programs at Excelsior College (Albany, NY). Previous to that, she was the Online Courses Manager at the Institute for Exploration and Development Geosciences and Director of Curriculum Development for the College of Liberal Studies, University of Oklahoma, Norman, OK, where she developed an online degree program curriculum for online courses at The University of Oklahoma. She also developed an interface for courses, as well as administrative and procedural support, support programmers, protocol and training manuals, and marketing approaches. She obtained her Ph.D. and M.A. in English and a B.S. in Geology from the University of Oklahoma. Nash blogs at E-Learning Queen (http://www.elearningqueen.com) and E-Learners, and has written articles and chapters on mobile learning, poetics, contemporary culture, and e-learning for numerous publications, including Trends and Issues in Instructional Design and Technology (3rd ed), Mobile Information Communication Technologies Adoption in Developing Countries: Effects and Implications, Talisman, Press1, International Journal of Learning Objects, GHR, World Literature, Gargoyle. Her latest books include Moodle 1.9 Teaching Techniques (Packt Publishing, 2010), E-Learners Survival Guide (Texture Press, 2009), and Klub Dobrih Dejanj (2008).

www.PacktPub.com

Support files, eBooks, discount offers and more

You might want to visit www.PacktPub.com for support files and downloads related to your book.

Did you know that Packt offers eBook versions of every book published, with PDF and ePub files available? You can upgrade to the eBook version at www.PacktPub.com and as a print book customer, you are entitled to a discount on the eBook copy. Get in touch with us at service@packtpub.com for more details.

At www.PacktPub.com, you can also read a collection of free technical articles, sign up for a range of free newsletters and receive exclusive discounts and offers on Packt books and eBooks.

http://PacktLib.PacktPub.com

Do you need instant solutions to your IT questions? PacktLib is Packt's online digital book library. Here, you can access, read and search across Packt's entire library of books.

Why Subscribe?

- ▸ Fully searchable across every book published by Packt
- ▸ Copy and paste, print and bookmark content
- ▸ On demand and accessible via web browser

Free Access for Packt account holders

If you have an account with Packt at www.PacktPub.com, you can use this to access PacktLib today and view nine entirely free books. Simply use your login credentials for immediate access.

Table of Contents

Preface

Moodle is the best e-learning solution on the block and is revolutionizing courses on the Web. Using JavaScript in Moodle is very useful for administrators and dynamic developers, as it uses built-in libraries to provide the modern and dynamic experience that is expected by web users today.

The Moodle JavaScript Cookbook will take you through the basics of combining Moodle with JavaScript and its various libraries and explain how JavaScript can be used along with Moodle. It will explain how to integrate Yahoo! User Interface Library (YUI) with Moodle. YUI will be the main focus of the book, and is the key to implementing modern, dynamic, feature-rich interfaces to help your users get a more satisfying and productive Moodle experience. It will enable you to add effects, make forms more responsive, use AJAX and animation, all to create a richer user experience. You will be able to work through a range of YUI features, such as pulling in and displaying information from other websites, enhancing existing UI elements to make users' lives easier, and even adding animation to your pages for a nice finishing touch.

What this book covers

Chapter 1, Combining Moodle and JavaScript. In this chapter, we will learn the basic techniques for integrating our JavaScript code with Moodle 2.0. We will learn several methods of including our JavaScript code in a Moodle page through .js files, and how to get the code to run. Lastly, we will look at some best practices and also how to make Moodle data and language strings available to our JavaScript code.

Chapter 2, Moodle and Yahoo! User Interface Library (YUI). In this chapter, we will learn the basics of working with YUI. We will learn how to initialize the YUI and make it ready for use within our code and load additional modules from both Version 2 and 3 of the YUI. We will also learn how to manage the execution of code by attaching events to our controls, and finally how to debug our code with YUI logging tools.

Chapter 3, Moodle Forms Validation. Moodle provides a feature-rich web forms utility based on the **PHP Extension and Application Repository** (**PEAR**) library, **QuickForm**. Forms produced in Moodle not using this library are an exception. So, in this chapter, we will learn how to activate the built-in JavaScript form validation functions, and also how to add our own custom JavaScript form validation logic.

Chapter 4, Manipulating Data with YUI 3. In this chapter, we will look at the ways in which we can use JavaScript and YUI to retrieve and display data from a range of different sources. Using these techniques, we can integrate all types of data into our Moodle applications—from weather forecasts, stock updates, and news feeds to any type of custom text-based data you may have from external systems, and even data from Moodle itself (both the local Moodle system and any remote systems that your code is authorized to access), retrieved through Moodle's web services API.

Chapter 5, Working with Data Tables. Database driven applications, such as Moodle require efficient methods of displaying data to users, for example a table of assignment grades, or other recent user activity. This typically takes the form of an HTML table, the familiar grid of columns and rows in the style of a spreadsheet. So in this chapter, we will learn how to initialize a YUI DataSource, display data, sort columns, add paging, and enable scrolling and editing.

Chapter 6, Enhancing Page Elements. The Yahoo! UI Library (YUI) offers a range of widgets and utilities to bring modern enhancements to your traditional page elements. In this chapter, we will look at a selection of these, including features often seen on modern interactive interfaces such as auto-complete, auto-update, custom tooltips, and so on.

Chapter 7, Advanced Layout Techniques. In this chapter, we will look at a selection of techniques available that are designed to enhance the way in which users interact with our content. First of all, we will look at the different ways in which we can present a navigation menu, giving the user a convenient list of the content that we are making available to them. Secondly, we will look at two different ways in which we can present the actual content to which they have navigated. We will also look at methods of enhancing the display and navigation of page content, by extending existing markup in keeping with the concept of "progressive enhancement".

Chapter 8, Animating Components. Animation can provide beneficial effects in a range of situations. So, in this chapter, we will look at how to bring elements on our pages to life with the use of animation.

Chapter 9, Integrating External Libraries. In this chapter, we will look at the methods available to us for integrating external JavaScript libraries. We will also look at how to setup some of the more commonly used frameworks, and implement a basic "content ready" event handler for each one. Finally, we will look at some extensions for the Prototype framework, namely the `script.aculo.us` add-on, and we will finish by implementing the Lightbox image-viewer extension.

What you need for this book

To work with the code provided with the recipes in this book, you will need an installation of Moodle 2.0 to run the code along with your favorite text editor for making any changes. Visit `http://moodle.org/` for downloading links and installation instructions for Moodle 2.0.

Who this book is for

This book is aimed at developers and administrators comfortable with customizing Moodle with the use of plugin modules, themes, and patches who want to make their site more dynamic. If you have prior knowledge of HTML, PHP, and CSS and a good working knowledge of the underlying structure of Moodle, then this book is for you. No prior experience with JavaScript is needed.

Conventions

In this book, you will find a number of styles of text that distinguish between different kinds of information. Here are some examples of these styles, and an explanation of their meaning.

Code words in text are shown as follows: "We will create a simple MooTools script that will display a JavaScript alert when the `domready` event is fired."

A block of code is set as follows:

```
window.addEvent('domready', function() {
    alert('Hello from MooTools');
});
```

When we wish to draw your attention to a particular part of a code block, the relevant lines or items are set in bold:

```
{
  key: "title",
  label: "Title",
  formatter: "string",
  sortable: true
}
```

New terms and **important words** are shown in bold. Words that you see on the screen, in menus or dialog boxes for example, appear in the text like this: "When the user clicks on the **Show panel** button, the window's `show` method is called".

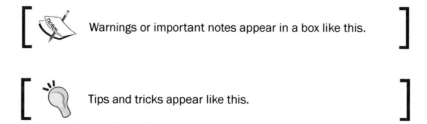

[Warnings or important notes appear in a box like this.]

[Tips and tricks appear like this.]

Reader feedback

Feedback from our readers is always welcome. Let us know what you think about this book—what you liked or may have disliked. Reader feedback is important for us to develop titles that you really get the most out of.

To send us general feedback, simply send an e-mail to `feedback@packtpub.com`, and mention the book title via the subject of your message.

If there is a book that you need and would like to see us publish, please send us a note in the **SUGGEST A TITLE** form on `www.packtpub.com` or e-mail `suggest@packtpub.com`.

If there is a topic that you have expertise in and you are interested in either writing or contributing to a book, see our author guide on `www.packtpub.com/authors`.

Customer support

Now that you are the proud owner of a Packt book, we have a number of things to help you to get the most from your purchase.

Downloading the example code

You can download the example code files for all Packt books you have purchased from your account at `http://www.PacktPub.com`. If you purchased this book elsewhere, you can visit `http://www.PacktPub.com/support` and register to have the files e-mailed directly to you.

Errata

Although we have taken every care to ensure the accuracy of our content, mistakes do happen. If you find a mistake in one of our books—maybe a mistake in the text or the code—we would be grateful if you would report this to us. By doing so, you can save other readers from frustration and help us improve subsequent versions of this book. If you find any errata, please report them by visiting http://www.packtpub.com/support, selecting your book, clicking on the **errata submission form** link, and entering the details of your errata. Once your errata are verified, your submission will be accepted and the errata will be uploaded on our website, or added to any list of existing errata, under the Errata section of that title. Any existing errata can be viewed by selecting your title from http://www.packtpub.com/support.

Piracy

Piracy of copyright material on the Internet is an ongoing problem across all media. At Packt, we take the protection of our copyright and licenses very seriously. If you come across any illegal copies of our works, in any form, on the Internet, please provide us with the location address or website name immediately so that we can pursue a remedy.

Please contact us at copyright@packtpub.com with a link to the suspected pirated material.

We appreciate your help in protecting our authors, and our ability to bring you valuable content.

Questions

You can contact us at questions@packtpub.com if you are having a problem with any aspect of the book, and we will do our best to address it.

1
Combining Moodle and JavaScript

In this chapter, we will cover:

- ▸ Creating a new Moodle PHP page
- ▸ Loading a JavaScript file
- ▸ Loading a JavaScript file in `<head>`
- ▸ Generating a JavaScript function call from PHP
- ▸ Passing variables from PHP to JavaScript
- ▸ Ensuring compliance with XHTML Strict
- ▸ Retrieving language strings from Moodle

Introduction

Web pages and websites have come a long way since their inception in the early 1990s (with the creation of HTML). Modern web applications such as Moodle now have far more in common with desktop applications than with the simple word processing documents they originally modeled.

One key weapon in the modern web application's armory is the subject of this book—JavaScript.

In essence, JavaScript is a programming language that runs in a user's web browser rather than on the web server. It allows programmers to manipulate the web page via what is called the **Document Object Model** (**DOM**). The DOM is a representation of the underlying HTML page, structured in a way to provide access to each and every element within the HTML page. Modern browsers now implement a standard version of the DOM, so it can be considered a cross-platform technology.

In recent years, there has been a significant uptake of the use of JavaScript frameworks. A JavaScript framework is a library of JavaScript code that makes a JavaScript programmer's life easier. Generally, they provide more efficient methods for performing the most common tasks in JavaScript, such as locating DOM elements or wiring up events to those elements. (An event is a function of an element. For example, an HTML input button element has a "click" event that is fired when the mouse is clicked while the pointer is over the button.) Additionally, they provide an abstraction of browser-specific quirks, making it very easy to write cross-platform code that works in the widest range of browsers.

One such JavaScript framework is the Yahoo! User Interface library (YUI). YUI is the framework of choice for Moodle 2.0, and is included with the standard Moodle 2.0 package. For this reason, a substantial number of techniques covered in the later chapters will be based on the YUI. In the final chapter, we will briefly explore some other popular JavaScript frameworks and libraries.

Perhaps more important than "how" to use JavaScript is the question of "when" to use it. It is vital to consider the target audience of your web applications and infer from this exactly how you will use JavaScript.

If you are building a web application that is to be widely used in a public setting, then you should aim to make it as accessible as possible to all types of users. With respect to JavaScript specifically, this means that the core functionality of your site should be available to those who, for whatever reason, cannot or will not use a browser that fully supports JavaScript (typical examples include a mobile device which has limited functionality, or a browser using automated text-to-speech or screen-reading software). These techniques form a part of what is known as "progressive enhancement".

In this first chapter, we will learn the basic techniques for integrating our JavaScript code with Moodle 2.0. We will learn several methods of including our JavaScript code in a Moodle page via .js files, and how to get the code to run. Lastly, we will look at some best practices and also how to make Moodle data and language strings available to our JavaScript code.

Creating a new Moodle PHP page

The code examples used in the recipes throughout this book are all based on the template we will create in this recipe. This template sets up the necessary Moodle environment and displays the standard Moodle header and footer.

This will allow us to look at the generic tools and techniques available to us within Moodle that pertain to JavaScript, allowing you, as the developer, to decide how and where to apply them.

In most instances, it is highly recommended to work with Moodle's rich plugin infrastructure to extend any functionality. This allows you to keep your enhancements completely separate from the core of Moodle, preventing you from introducing bugs into the core code, and making the Moodle upgrade process just a case of ensuring that your particular plugin folders are copied into the upgraded Moodle installation.

Please refer to the Moodle documentation at `http://docs.moodle.org/` to decide which plugin framework suits your requirements.

There may be rare cases when it is simply not possible to implement the functionality you desire inside the plugin frameworks, requiring the modification of core code. If this is the case, it is likely that the functionality you desire will be useful to all Moodle users. Therefore, you should look to engage with the Moodle development community to seek advice regarding the feasibility of having your changes included in the next revision of the core code.

If, however, you know for a fact that you definitely need to make changes to core code and that those changes will only be useful to your bespoke use of Moodle, you may consider (as a last resort) modifying the core code files. Be aware that this method is not without issues, incurring significant disadvantages, such as:

- Keeping track of each change you make to each file, and merging these changes as you upgrade to future versions of Moodle. Version control systems such as CVS or GIT may assist you here.

- Your changes will not be subject to the same standard of testing and debugging as that of the official core code.

- Your changes will not be guaranteed to continue to work in future versions; you will need to fully test your changes with each future upgrade.

So, as you can see, there is a trade-off in functionality versus maintainability for each method of extending and enhancing Moodle; so you should choose wisely. If in doubt, use a plugin or theme!

Getting ready

To begin with, we will create a subfolder named `cook` within our Moodle installation where we will put all the files we will work with throughout the book.

Next we will create the template PHP file `blank.php`, with the following content:

```php
<?php
require_once(dirname(__FILE__) . '/../config.php');
$PAGE->set_context(get_context_instance(CONTEXT_SYSTEM));
$PAGE->set_url('/cook/blank.php');
echo $OUTPUT->header();
echo $OUTPUT->footer();
?>
```

Downloading the example code

We now have our template saved at `/path/to/moodle/cook/blank.php`.

To test this new template, we can load it in a web browser and check if all is well. Assuming we have a web server running with Moodle served at the base URL `http://localhost/moodle`, we can load the following URL to test our new template: `http://localhost/moodle/cook/blank.php`.

If the template is set up correctly, we will see a basic page with standard header and footer, similar to the following:

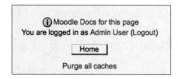

How to do it...

We begin by opening the PHP tags in the standard way, using `<?php`.

Note that we have not used the shorthand notation of `<?`, as this goes against the Moodle programming guidelines and also against general good practice.

Next, we must include Moodle's global configuration file. The inclusion of this file sets up the requisite Moodle programming environment, including two global variables we will make use of: `$PAGE` and `$OUTPUT`.

`$PAGE` is defined as a central store of information about the current page we are generating in response to the user's request.

The `$PAGE` object allows us to start defining the properties of the page, namely the context and the URL. The context of the page is the scope of the page, that is, where in the Moodle system it is being used. We are using the **System** context; other examples are in the **Course** or **Module** context.

Next, we set the URL of the page. This mirrors our directory structure; so in this case we just set it to `/cook/blank.php`.

`$OUTPUT` is defined as an instance of `core_renderer` or one of its subclasses. Use it to generate HTML for output.

The `$OUTPUT` object allows us to generate the `header` and `footer` for our page, based on the current Moodle theme. This is done by calling the header and footer methods of the `$OUTPUT` object, and using echo to write them to the page.

How it works...

After opening the PHP tag, we can begin inserting the PHP code. We use `require_once` to include the Moodle configuration file (this ensures that the file is included only once, and will halt execution of the page if the file is unavailable). The path to the configuration file is determined by using the `dirname` function to get the directory path to the current file (using the built-in `__FILE__` constant), and then traversing up one directory (as we are in our `cook` subdirectory) to find the `config.php` file.

Next, we set the page context by calling the `set_context` method of the `$PAGE` object. This takes a context instance. We retrieve the instance for the system context by passing the `CONTEXT_SYSTEM` constant to the `get_context_instance` function.

The final usage of the `$PAGE` object is to set the page URL, which is done using the `set_url` method, passing in a web root relative URL path, which is `/cook/blank.php` in this case.

Next, we need to use the `$OUTPUT` object to generate the header and footer of the page. Both header and footer methods return HTML as a string, so we can use the `echo` construct to write these strings to the page.

Loading a JavaScript file

A majority of the JavaScript we add will be contained within an external JavaScript file, which is a text file with a `.js` extension. In this recipe, we will learn how to use the `$PAGE` object to include such a file.

Getting ready

Make a new PHP file named `requirejs.php` in the `cook` directory similar to the template in the previous recipe:

```php
<?php
require_once(dirname(__FILE__) . '/../config.php');

$PAGE->set_context(get_context_instance(CONTEXT_SYSTEM));
$PAGE->set_url('/cook/requirejs.php');
$PAGE->requires->js('/cook/alert.js');
echo $OUTPUT->header();
echo $OUTPUT->footer();
?>
```

Next, we create the accompanying JavaScript file, `alert.js`, with the following content:

```javascript
alert('Hello World!');
```

Now when we load the page in a web browser, we see that the JavaScript alert is displayed as shown in the following screenshot, proving to us that our code has loaded and executed correctly:

Note that we see the **Home** button, meaning that the footer of the page has loaded. This is because our code is executed at the end of the <body> tag.

How to do it...

We have created a page based on the blank template we created in the first recipe of this chapter. To this, we have added the following line:

```
$PAGE->requires->js('/cook/alert.js');
```

How it works...

We are making use of the Page Requirements Manager, $PAGE, which is an object that contains various methods for setting up additional components for a page. Here we have called the $PAGE->requires->js method, and passed the path to our .js file as a parameter.

Moodle then adds this script to the list of scripts to be included within the final rendered page. A <script> tag similar to the following will be inserted just before the closing <body> tag:

```
<script type="text/javascript"
  src="http://localhost/moodle/lib/javascript.php?
  file=%2Fcook%2Falert.js&amp;rev=1"></script>
```

 The <script> tag is inserted at the end of the <body> tag, inline with the current best practice, offering the best page performance and a simplification of handling DOM-ready events among other reasons. For a fuller discussion of this technique, please refer to the Yahoo! Developer Network resource at the following URL:

http://developer.yahoo.com/performance/rules.html#js_bottom

This code **must** be included **after** the Moodle configuration file config.php has been included. This is where the $PAGE object is setup for us.

Loading a JavaScript file in <head>

In the previous recipe we learned the standard method of including a JavaScript file at the end of the document's <body> tag.

In this recipe, we will look at how to ensure our JavaScript file is included within the <head> tag. There are numerous reasons why you would require your file be included within the <head>, for example if you need to use document.write to manually write <head> content.

 If you are in any doubt, use the technique in the previous recipe. If you need to use the technique in this recipe, the chances are you will know exactly why.

Getting ready

Once again, open the Moodle PHP file where we will add our .js file. We will use the simple example from the previous recipe as a basis, with the necessary changes:

```php
<?php
require_once(dirname(__FILE__) . '/../config.php');
$PAGE->set_context(get_context_instance(CONTEXT_SYSTEM));
$PAGE->requires->js('/cook/alert.js', true);
$PAGE->set_url('/cook/requirejs_head.php');
echo $OUTPUT->header();
echo $OUTPUT->footer();
?>
```

Now when we load the page, we see that our JavaScript alert is executed immediately, assuring us that our code is loading and executing correctly, as seen in the following screenshot:

The page at http://localhost says:

Hello World!

OK

Note that the page underneath is blank at this stage, as our JavaScript code is being run from the <head> tag, before the rest of the page has loaded.

How to do it...

You will notice that this code is almost identical to that of the previous recipe. The key difference here is the parameters we have passed to the $PAGE->requires->js method. We have passed a second optional parameter which determines whether or not the <script> tag will be rendered within the document's <head> tag. In this case, we set it to true to ensure that the <script> tag is rendered as such.

How it works...

We have called $PAGE->requires->js again, this time with two parameters. The first is the path to the .js file we wish to include. The second is a Boolean value which specifies whether or not to include the file from within the <head> tag of the HTML page.

The <script> tag that is rendered to the document is identical to that of the previous recipe, with the crucial difference that it is rendered within the <head> tag, rather than at the end of the <body> tag.

Generating a JavaScript function call from PHP

Now that we have loaded our JavaScript file, we need a method to execute that code. Once again, we may use the Page Requirements Manager $PAGE to generate a call to our JavaScript function.

 This recipe describes a basic technique for executing your JavaScript code when the page is loaded. More sophisticated techniques based on handling DOM events with the Yahoo! User Interface library will be covered in later chapters.

Getting ready

Set up a page requirejs_init.php with the following content:

```php
<?php

    require_once(dirname(__FILE__) . '/../config.php');
    $PAGE->set_context(get_context_instance(CONTEXT_SYSTEM));
    $PAGE->set_url('/cook/requirejs_init.php');
    $PAGE->requires->js('/cook/requirejs_init.js');
    $PAGE->requires->js_init_call('hello');
    echo $OUTPUT->header();
    echo $OUTPUT->footer();

?>
```

Set up the accompanying JavaScript file, `requirejs_init.js`, with the following content:

```
function hello(Y)
{
  alert('Hello World!');
}
```

Now when we load the page, we see that our JavaScript alert is executed, assuring us that our code is loading and executing correctly, as seen in the following screenshot:

How to do it...

We wish to make a call to our JavaScript function named `hello`. This is achieved with the `js_init_call` method. We pass one parameter, which is a string containing the name of the function we wish to call, which is `hello`.

How it works...

When the document is rendered, the `js_init_call` method ensures that a call to our JavaScript function is generated. This example will generate the following JavaScript:

```
hello(Y);
```

This JavaScript is then included inside a `<script>` tag at the end of the `<body>` tag of the final page.

Passing variables from PHP to JavaScript

In the previous recipe, we learned how to run our JavaScript function, but we did not pass any data to it. In this recipe, we will pass two parameters to the JavaScript function—a message to be displayed and the current user's username, demonstrating how to make variable values from PHP available within our JavaScript code.

Getting ready

Create a new PHP file `requirejs_init_data.php` with the following content:

```php
<?php

    require_once(dirname(__FILE__) . '/../config.php');
    $PAGE->set_context(get_context_instance(CONTEXT_SYSTEM));
    $PAGE->set_url('/cook/requirejs_init_data.php');
    $PAGE->requires->js('/cook/requirejs_init_data.js');

    $PAGE->requires->js_init_call('hello',
    array('Hello', $USER->username));

    echo $OUTPUT->header();
    echo $OUTPUT->footer();

?>
```

This code sets up a simple Moodle page and includes a JavaScript file `requirejs_init_ data.js` containing the following basic "Hello World" function that we will call, which accepts three parameters.

Note that the first parameter `Y`, which is an instance of the YUI object, is automatically passed to our function by the Page Requirements Manager.

The two subsequent parameters are strings to be passed to the function: `message` and `username`:

```
function hello(Y,message,username)
{
   alert(message + ', ' + username);
}
```

Now when we load the page, we see that our JavaScript alert is executed, displaying the message we passed along with the current user's username (**admin**):

How to do it...

Just after the call to $PAGE->requires->js, add the following code:

```
$PAGE->requires->js_init_call('hello',
    array('Hello', $USER->username));
```

The first parameter is a string containing the name of the JavaScript function we wish to call, which is hello in this case.

The second parameter is a PHP array of values that are passed on to the JavaScript function in the order in which they are defined.

The use of an array here allows the js_init_call method to support an arbitrary number of arguments, two in this case: the message and username.

How it works...

We have used the Page Requirement Manager to register the name of the function we wish to be called and passed two additional parameters required by the function inside a PHP array.

When the document is rendered, the following JavaScript will be generated inside a <script> tag just before the end of the <body> tag:

```
hello(Y, "Hello", "admin");
```

Ensuring compliance with XHTML Strict

Moodle uses the DocType XHTML Strict. We should take care to ensure our JavaScript maintains compliance with this standard.

Although it is best avoided, it may occasionally be necessary to include JavaScript code within <script> tags that are embedded within the page. If this is the case, it is highly likely that the code will include characters that have special meaning to the XHTML Strict specification, for example & and < ', ' > to name a few.

Getting ready

Open the PHP file that contains the embedded JavaScript and locate the start and end <script> tags.

How to do it...

Add the following code immediately after the opening `<script>` tag:

```
<script language="JavaScript" type="text/javascript">
//<![CDATA[
```

Add the following code immediately before the closing `<script>` tag:

```
//]]>
</script>
```

How it works...

The CDATA tag we have used informs the XHTML rendering engine that it should treat anything inside as arbitrary data, and not to attempt to parse it as if it were valid XHTML markup.

Additionally, to avoid a conflict with JavaScript syntax, the lines on which the CDATA tags reside have been commented out with double forward slashes (`//`).

Retrieving language strings from Moodle

Moodle makes extensive use of language strings to support full multilingual internationalization. In practice, this means that strings which are used within the interface are held in language-specific files. For example, the string "Submit assignment" may be held in the relevant English language file, and this string may be referred to indirectly via a short name key.

This makes it trivial to support additional languages by creating files for those languages. As the code refers to the strings via their short name keys, it is easy to simply switch the set of language files, and the code will pick up the strings in the new preferred language. This happens automatically when a user changes their preferred language settings.

When providing textual feedback to the user from our JavaScript code, we should make use of Moodle's language string system. This ensures our code is inherently multilingual and makes it easy for a non-developer to provide a language translation of our module.

Getting ready

In this example, we will retrieve the built-in Moodle language string `course` and show that it is available from our JavaScript code by displaying it with the alert function.

We start once again with a basic Moodle page and associated `.js` file:

```
<?php
  require_once(dirname(__FILE__) . '/../config.php');
```

```
    $PAGE->set_context(get_context_instance(CONTEXT_SYSTEM));
    $PAGE->set_url('/cook/requirejs_init_lang.php');
    $PAGE->requires->js('/cook/requirejs_init_lang.js');
    $PAGE->requires->string_for_js('course', 'moodle');
    $PAGE->requires->js_init_call('lang');

    echo $OUTPUT->header();
    echo $OUTPUT->footer();
?>
```

As you can see, this code registers a call to the function `lang` which has been defined in the associated `.js` file:

```
function lang(Y)
{
    alert(M.str.moodle.course);
}
```

Now when we load the page, we see that our JavaScript alert is executed, displaying the language string value we set up, as seen in the following screenshot:

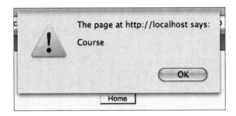

How to do it...

We have included our `.js` with the method now familiar—`$PAGE->requires->js`.

After this line comes a new feature of the Page Requirements Manager, the `string_for_js` function:

```
    $PAGE->requires->string_for_js('course', 'moodle');
```

Finally, we refer to this language string from our JavaScript code:

```
    alert(M.str.moodle.course);
```

How it works...

We call the `string_for_js` method with two parameters: the name of the string we wish to retrieve and the location of this string. In this example, we are retrieving the language string for `course` from the core Moodle language file.

Now this string is made available to us as part of Moodle's global JavaScript namespace (M) in the format, `M.str.<module name>.<string name>`. In our example, this is `M.str.moodle.course`.

Using this method, the strings we have set up will be available to all subsequent JavaScript code. If we had simply passed this string as a parameter to the JavaScript function, it would only be available inside that function. If we required it to be available within additional functions, we would have to repeat the process, making copies of the string and passing those to the additional functions resulting in unnecessarily inefficient code.

2

Moodle and Yahoo! User Interface Library (YUI)

In this chapter, we will cover:

- Initializing the YUI 3 library
- Loading YUI 3 modules
- Loading YUI 2 modules from YUI 3
- Attaching basic event handlers
- Attaching advanced DOM event handlers
- Implementing Event Delegation
- Debugging with the YUI console

Introduction

There are a lot of common tasks that need to be performed when writing JavaScript. A large proportion of this simply involves dealing with differences between web browsers. The need for a way to hide or abstract the specifics of each browser into a standard interface gave rise to sets of tools known as JavaScript libraries. One of the leading libraries in use on the web today is the **Yahoo! User Interface Library** (**YUI**).

Moodle includes a copy of the YUI as its preferred JavaScript library. YUI provides developers with access to a wide range of tools for enhancing their web applications:

> *The YUI Library is a set of utilities and controls, written with JavaScript and CSS, for building richly interactive web applications using techniques such as DOM scripting, DHTML and AJAX. YUI is available under a BSD license and is free for all uses.*
> *YUI is* **proven, scalable, fast,** *and* **robust.** *Built by frontend engineers at Yahoo! and contributors from around the world, it's an industrial-strength JavaScript library for professionals who love JavaScript.*
>
> *Yahoo! Developer Network*
> `http://developer.yahoo.com/yui/`

In this chapter, we will learn the basics of working with YUI. We will learn how to initialize the YUI and make it ready for use within our code and load additional modules from versions 2 and 3 of the YUI. We will also learn how to manage the execution of code by attaching events to our controls, and finally how to debug our code with YUI logging tools.

Initializing the YUI 3 library

In this recipe, we will learn how to initialize the YUI 3 environment within Moodle, which will get us ready to start using YUI 3 features. Moodle takes care of most of the initial setup, namely loading the required CSS and JavaScript files, so all we need to be concerned with is activating the YUI environment.

This example will show how to execute JavaScript code from within the YUI environment. We will set up a small YUI script which will simply display a message including the version number of the active YUI environment in a JavaScript alert box.

This provides a simple view of what is required to get YUI up and running that we will build on further in the subsequent recipes.

Getting ready

We begin by setting up a new PHP file `yui_init.php` in the `cook` directory with the following content:

```php
<?php
    require_once(dirname(__FILE__) . '/../config.php');
    $PAGE->set_context(get_context_instance(CONTEXT_SYSTEM));
    $PAGE->set_url('/cook/yui_init.php');
    $PAGE->requires->js('/cook/yui_init.js');
    echo $OUTPUT->header();
    echo $OUTPUT->footer();
?>
```

Notice that the preceding code references a JavaScript file `yui_init.js`, which has the following content:

```
YUI().use
(
  function(Y)
  {
    alert('Hello from YUI ' + Y.version);
  }
);
```

How to do it...

We have created a PHP file that sets up a Moodle programming environment and includes a JavaScript file, in a way now familiar to us from previous recipes.

What is new here is the content of the JavaScript file, which is where we will make ready the YUI 3 environment.

Moodle has already included all the JavaScript files required for YUI (this happened when we output the value returned from `$OUTPUT->header();`). This means we now have a global object named `YUI` available within our JavaScript code.

We create a new instance of the `YUI` object with the statement `YUI()` and then immediately call the `use` method.

The only parameter we will pass to the `use` method is an anonymous function. This is just like a regular JavaScript function, except that it has no name specified; hence it is "anonymous". A name is not required, as it is not referred to again, but it is simply passed directly to the `use` method. This function itself accepts a single input parameter `Y`, which will be a reference to the new instance of the `YUI` object. (Note that the `use` method is also used to load additional YUI modules; this is the subject of the next recipe.)

The anonymous function just created is the most important part of the code to take note of as this is where we will be putting our entire code that will be making use of the YUI features. In this example, you can see that we are just creating a JavaScript alert with a short message including the value of `Y.version`, which is simply a string containing the version number of YUI that has been loaded as seen in the following screenshot:

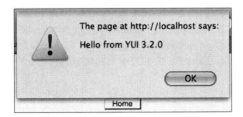

Here, we can see that our code has successfully initialized the YUI 3.2.0 environment and is ready for us to start using the features available within the YUI and its additional modules.

How it works...

We have created a new instance of the global object YUI, and called the use method, passing in an anonymous function that contains the code we wish to run. When the new instance of the YUI object is fully loaded, it makes a call to our anonymous function, and our code is executed.

In this example, our code displays a short message containing the version number of the YUI instance we created, confirming that we have a fully functional YUI 3 environment as a basis to implement further YUI features.

Loading additional YUI modules

YUI has a whole host of additional modules providing a very wide range of functionalities. Some examples of commonly used functionalities provided by additional modules include:

- Animation
- Drag and drop
- Manipulating DOM elements
- Handling DOM events (that is an input button's "click" event)
- Handling data (JSON/XML)

For a current list of all the modules available, please refer to the Yahoo! Developer Network website for YUI 3 at the URL: `http://developer.yahoo.com/yui/3/`

How to do it...

The loading of additional modules is achieved via the use method of the YUI object. In the previous recipe we learned how to run code via the use method with the following syntax:

```
YUI().use
( function(Y) { /* <code to execute> */ } );
```

Note that the use method takes an arbitrarily long number of arguments (one or more) and only the last argument must be the anonymous function described in the previous recipe. The preceding arguments are a list of one or more modules you wish to load. So for example, to load the Animation module (anim) and the DOM Event Utility module (event), we would use the following syntax in place of the preceding one:

```
YUI().use
( "anim", "event", function(Y) { /* <code to execute> */ } );
```

Now all of the features of these two additional modules (`anim` and `event`) will be available within the anonymous function that contains the code we want to execute.

This technique will be used to load the modules we require in the examples contained in the subsequent recipes.

Loading YUI 2 modules from YUI 3

There can be several reasons why we would want to load YUI 2 modules from within YUI 3. We may have a substantial amount of pre-written YUI 2 code that we wish to use straight away, saving us the trouble of rewriting it from scratch. Another reason may be, as in this book, we wish to use features of the YUI 2 that have not yet been re-implemented as native YUI 3 modules.

In this recipe, we will learn how to load YUI 2 modules from within YUI 3 by loading the Calendar widget from YUI 2, inside a native YUI 3 script.

Getting ready

We begin by creating a new PHP file `yui_cal.php` in the `cook` directory with the following content:

```php
<?php
require_once(dirname(__FILE__) . '/../config.php');

$PAGE->set_context(get_context_instance(CONTEXT_SYSTEM));
$PAGE->set_url('/cook/yui_cal.php');
$PAGE->requires->js('/cook/yui_cal.js');

echo $OUTPUT->header();

?>
<div id="calContainer"></div>
<?php
echo $OUTPUT->footer();
?>
```

You will notice that `yui_cal.php` links to a JavaScript file `yui_cal.js`, also in the `cook` directory, with the following content:

```javascript
YUI().use("yui2-calendar", function(Y)
{
  var YAHOO = Y.YUI2;
  var cal = new YAHOO.widget.Calendar("calContainer");
  cal.render();
});
```

How to do it...

First, we created a PHP file, `yui_cal.php` in which we set up the Moodle programming environment and included our JavaScript file, `yui_cal.js`. Also, in this PHP file we have included a container `<div>` tag to which we have assigned the ID `calContainer`. As you may have guessed, this will be where we will render the YUI 2 calendar control.

Moving on to the JavaScript portion of this recipe contained in `yui_cal.js`, we have first loaded the module named `yui2-calendar`. All available YUI 2 modules are referenced using their original names prefixed with `yui2-`. So `calendar` becomes `yui2-calendar`.

The next step is to recreate the `YAHOO` object from YUI 2. This is available as part of the YUI 3 object `Y`, in the form of `Y.YUI2`. For convenience, we will copy this into a new object named `YAHOO`. As this now matches the YUI 2 coding style, it makes it easy for us to reuse existing YUI 2 code here.

Finally, we create a new instance of the YUI 2 calendar widget `YAHOO.widget.Calendar`, passing in the ID of the container `<div>` we created earlier, and then call the `render` method to display the calendar.

Our page should now have a new calendar control rendered inside our `<div>` container as seen in the following screenshot:

How it works...

When we load `yui_cal.php` in a web browser, our page is rendered including the container `<div>` for our calendar. When the page has finished downloading, our JavaScript is executed.

From our JavaScript, the YUI 2 Calendar module is loaded first by YUI 3 in the same way it loads YUI 3 modules, the difference being we have used the name of a YUI 2 module prefixed with `yui2-`, that is, `yui2-calendar`.

Next, we have obtained a copy of the YUI 2 object `YAHOO` by copying it from the YUI 3 object `Y.YUI2`.

Finally, we can use the new YAHOO object to create a new instance of the Calendar widget, attaching it to our container <div> and calling the render method to have it built and displayed.

Attaching basic event handlers

Events are the basis for managing how the user interface responds to particular actions taken by the user, primarily with the keyboard and/or mouse. An event is a particular action taken in the context of a particular DOM element. The following are two common examples:

- An input button element has a click event, which occurs when the user clicks the mouse while the mouse pointer is hovering over the button
- An input text box has a focus event, which occurs when the text box has gained focus, meaning the user has moved the cursor into the text box either with the mouse cursor or using the *Tab* key

Therefore, an event handler is a specific block of code (callback function) that we have registered (attached) to a particular element and event combination, that is, the input button and its click event.

In this recipe, we will learn how to attach a click event handler to an HTML input button as per the first example. We will set up the code such that an alert is displayed when the button is clicked.

Getting ready

We begin by creating a new PHP file yui_eventbasic.php in the cook directory, with the following content:

```php
<?php
  require_once(dirname(__FILE__) . '/../config.php');
  $PAGE->set_context(get_context_instance(CONTEXT_SYSTEM));
  $PAGE->set_url('/cook/yui_event.php');
  $PAGE->requires->js('/cook/yui_eventbasic.js');
  echo $OUTPUT->header();
?>
<form>
  <input type="button" id="btn1" value="Button 1" />
</form>
<?php
  echo $OUTPUT->footer();
?>
```

You will notice that `yui_eventbasic.php` links to a JavaScript file `yui_eventbasic.js`, also in the `cook` directory, with the following content:

```
YUI().use("node-base", function(Y) {
  var btn1_Click = function(e)
  {
    alert('Button clicked');
  };
  Y.on("click", btn1_Click, "#btn1");
});
```

How to do it...

We have set up the Moodle programming environment in the way now familiar in `yui_eventbasic.php`, with the addition of a form with an input button labeled **Button 1** with the ID `btn1` as seen in the following screenshot:

This is the button to which we shall register a click event, referring to it by its ID later on. This PHP file also includes the JavaScript file `yui_eventbasic.js` from where we will set up the event.

The JavaScript in `yui_eventbasic.js` begins by loading the module we require —`node-base`.

Next, we have defined a function `btn1_Click` which will serve as the click event handler. This function simply displays an alert to demonstrate that the event has fired correctly.

Lastly, we use the `on` method of the `Y` object to register the event, passing three parameters as detailed in the following table:

Parameter	Value
Name of the event	`click`
Name of the function to register	`btn1_Click`
ID of the element to which the event pertains	`#btn1`

Now we can load our PHP page in a web browser, and when we click on **Button 1**, we will see the JavaScript alert pop up, letting us know that the click event has fired correctly and called our event handler as seen in the following screenshot:

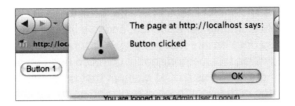

How it works...

When we built the PHP page including our input button, we assigned an ID to that button via the `id` attribute. This is what allows us to later refer to that button specifically from the JavaScript code.

When our page is loaded in the browser, our JavaScript file is also loaded and executed, initializing the YUI environment. Next, our function `btn1_Click` is defined.

Lastly, we used the `Y.on` method to assign this function to the click event of the button. The name of the event is simply "click" which all browsers understand. Our event handler is simply referenced by name, that is, `btn1_Click`. Lastly, we told `Y.on` to apply the event handler to the element with ID `btn1` by passing the ID prefixed with a #, that is, `#btn1`.

> `Y.on` uses a CSS selector syntax to refer to elements; hence the ID is prefixed with a # in the same way it would be if we were defining a CSS selector.
>
> This is a powerful and flexible method for registering events as we could alternatively use the identifier `.btn` which would then register this event handler for **all** elements with the class attribute set to `btn`.

Attaching advanced DOM event handlers

Sometimes we simply want to run JavaScript code when the page loads, rather than in response to an action taken by the user (as in the previous example).

A simple way to achieve this would be to put our code directly in the JavaScript file outside of any functions or event handlers. Using this method, our code would just be executed straight after it is loaded. If we are following the best practice technique of loading our script files at the end of the body tag, our code will be executed after the main body content of the page has loaded.

Note that Moodle implements this best practice for us automatically when we use the technique from the *Loading a JavaScript file* recipe in *Chapter 1, Combining Moodle and JavaScript* unless we specify otherwise, as per the *Loading a JavaScript file in the <head>* recipe. Using this latter technique of loading a script file from the `<head>`, our code would be executed before the rest of the page had finished loading.

This simple technique is sufficient for cases where the code we wish to execute does not depend upon certain DOM elements being loaded, and to a limited extent loading a script file at the end of the body tag does ensure that the page's DOM elements will be fully loaded and available to our code. However, this method cannot be relied upon across all web browsers. In some cases, our attempts to access a DOM element that is not fully loaded may cause the rest of our script to fail, and in the worst case, it may even cause an inferior web browser to crash! Obviously, this is far from ideal—enter YUI.

The YUI 3 library offers a set of significantly more robust solutions to this problem, which can be relied upon across all web browsers that the YUI supports. It is these offerings which we will investigate in this recipe, and they take the form of the events described in the following table:

Event	Description
domready	Fired when the page's DOM is fully loaded and can therefore be accessed safely. This element refers to the full DOM context of the page and is therefore not applied to a specific element.
load	Applied to a specific DOM element. It fires when that element is fully loaded by the browser. If applied to the window element, this fires when the entire contents of the window has loaded, including the page and any scripts, style sheets, or images.
available	Applied to a specific DOM element. It fires when the element has loaded, but not necessarily after the element's child elements have loaded.
contentready	Applied to a specific DOM element. It fires when the element and all of its child elements are fully loaded.

We will implement each of these four events in order to gain greater understanding of when they are fired, both relative to the page load lifecycle as a whole, and relative to each other. For each element, we will print a message numbered from one to four, reflecting the order in which they were fired. Note that this order varies from browser to browser.

Getting ready

We begin by creating a new PHP file yui_eventdom.php in the cook directory, with the following content:

```php
<?php
    require_once(dirname(__FILE__) . '/../config.php');

    $PAGE->set_context(get_context_instance(CONTEXT_SYSTEM));
    $PAGE->set_url('/cook/yui_event.php');
    $PAGE->requires->js('/cook/yui_eventdom.js');

    echo $OUTPUT->header();
?>
<div id="container">
```

```
  <h1>Events called, in order:</h1>
</div>
<?php
  echo $OUTPUT->footer();
?>
```

You will notice that yui_eventdom.php links to a JavaScript file yui_eventdom.js, also in the cook directory, with the following content:

```
YUI().use("node-base", function(Y)
{
  Y.on
  (
    "available",
    function()
    {
      printMessage("Element #container 'available'");
    },
    "#container"
  );

  Y.on
  (
    "contentready",
    function()
    {
      printMessage("Elememt #container 'contentready'");
    },
    "#container"
  );

  Y.on
  (
    "domready",
    function()
    {
      printMessage("Page 'domready'");
    }
  );

  Y.on
  (
    "load",
    function(e)
    {
      printMessage("Window 'load'");
    },
    Y.config.win
  );
```

```
    var order = 1;
    var container = Y.one('#container');
    function printMessage(message)
    {
        container.append('<p>' + order++ + '. ' + message + '</p>');
    }
});
```

How to do it...

In the PHP file `yui_eventdom.php`, we set up the standard Moodle programming environment as usual, and included a `<div>` tag, inside which we will print messages from each of the four event handlers. Note that we have set an ID `container` for this `<div>` tag, ensuring that we can reference it later on in our JavaScript.

Moving on to our JavaScript file `yui_eventdom.js`, we begin by loading the node-base module which gives us access to the `Y.on` method, which we will use to register the event handlers. Next, we set up the four event handlers we are demonstrating, beginning with `available` and `contentready`, which are registered in our container `<div>`. The next event handler is `domready`, which is not applied to any particular element as the DOM is intrinsic to the page. Finally, we register the load event to `Y.config.win`, which is YUI's browser-independent reference to the page's window object.

Inside each of these event handlers we have made a call to the function `printMessage`, which prints the message passed to it, along with a numbered prefix reflecting the order in which the call was made.

Now when we load our page in a web browser, we will see the order in which the events have been called. The order generally corresponds to the "safest" one first. That is, the order that allows the respective events to be called as early as possible in the page load lifecycle without running into any browser-specific issues such as crashes due to attempts to access DOM elements that have not been loaded.

In the following screenshots we can see how the order changes between three common web browsers:

▸ Safari 5

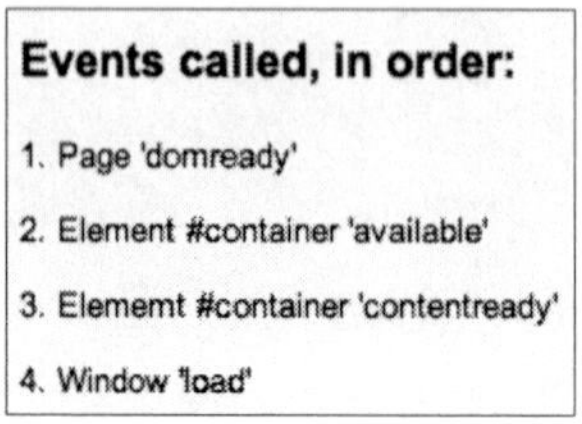

> **Events called, in order:**
>
> 1. Page 'domready'
>
> 2. Element #container 'available'
>
> 3. Elememt #container 'contentready'
>
> 4. Window 'load'

▸ Firefox 3

Events called, in order:

1. Element #container 'available'

2. Elememt #container 'contentready'

3. Page 'domready'

4. Window 'load'

▸ Internet Explorer 8

Events called, in order:

1. Window 'load'

2. Page 'domready'

3. Element #container 'available'

4. Elememt #container 'contentready'

Notice that Firefox 3 has the most intuitive order, with the container `<div>` tag first being **available**, and then **contentready** once its child elements have loaded. Next, the page is **domready**, and finally the window-load event is fired once all additional assets (scripts, stylesheets, and images) have loaded.

How it works...

We used the `Y.on` method to get YUI to assign the events to their respective elements. When the page is executed, YUI manages these in a browser-specific manner, firing our events at the earliest but safest possible opportunity.

When the events are fired, a call is made to our `printMessage` function, which prints that message, prefixed with a number indicating the order the event was fired in. This is achieved by keeping a count with the global variable `order`, which starts at `1`. Every time we print a message, we include this number in the text, and increase its value by one, ready for the next message to be displayed.

Implementing event delegation

So far we have looked at a range of methods for registering single events to single elements. These techniques are very useful but it becomes inefficient and laborious when we wish to register events for multiple elements.

If we take the example of a navigation control in the form of a list of links, we could implement a click event for each link by manually registering the event against the ID of the element. While this may be fine for a handful of links, as soon as the list starts to get larger it becomes very cumbersome to manage these events. The more links there are, the more it becomes prone to mistakes and bugs. Would you want to write (and manage) code to register click events to 50 links by hand if you didn't have to?

Fortunately, it so happens that the YUI has a solution for just this type of problem, namely Event Delegation.

Event delegation is a technique whereby we can designate a parent element to hand down events to its child elements. Picking up our example of a list of links, this means we can use the element containing our list to manage the events of the links in that list.

In this recipe, we will use event delegation to implement a click event handler for each one of a list of links. In the click event handler we will simply display an alert showing which link was clicked. Using this method we can add as many links into the list as we want at any time later on, avoiding the need to add or change any of our JavaScript code when we do so.

Getting ready

We start by creating a PHP file `yui_delegation.php` with the following content:

```php
<?php
  require_once(dirname(__FILE__) . '/../config.php');

  $PAGE->set_context(get_context_instance(CONTEXT_SYSTEM));
  $PAGE->set_url('/cook/yui_delegation.php');
  $PAGE->requires->js('/cook/yui_delegation.js');
  echo $OUTPUT->header();
?>
<div id="container">
  <ul>
    <li id="li-1"><a href="#">Item 1</a></li>
    <li id="li-2"><a href="#">Item 2</a></li>
    <li id="li-3"><a href="#">Item 3</a></li>
    <li id="li-4"><a href="#">Item 4</a></li>
    <li id="li-5"><a href="#">Item 5</a></li>
  </ul>
</div>
<?php
  echo $OUTPUT->footer();
?>
```

Next, we create the JavaScript file `yui_delegation.js` that was referenced in the `yui_delegation.php` file:

```
YUI().use("event-delegate", function(Y)
{
  Y.delegate("click", function (e)
  {
    var item = this.one('a').get('text');
    alert("You clicked " + item);
  }, "#container", "li");
});
```

How to do it...

We created a PHP page and set up the Moodle programming environment as usual. We included an unordered list of links inside a `<div>` container. It is for these links that we will implement click events via delegation.

Next, we move on to the JavaScript code, beginning by loading the `event-delegate` module that we require for this technique. This makes available a new method, `Y.delegate`.

Using `Y.delegate`, we then delegate the click events for the list items within our container `<div>`.

Finally, when we load the page in a web browser and click on one of the links, we see our message pop up, including the name of the item that we actually clicked on as seen in the following screenshot:

How it works...

After loading the `event-delegate` module, the `Y.delegate` method is available. `Y.delegate` takes four arguments:

Description	Value
The type of event to delegate	click
The function to register	The click handler function
The name of the parent element	#container
The child elements for the events	li

`Y.delegate` then sets up a click handler for all of the `li` elements within the `#container` element, and registers the function that we have passed.

Inside this function, the particular element that has fired the event is referred to as "this". In this case, "this" is an `<li>` object containing the `<a>` link tag. Here, we just read the text of the link tag and display it in a message to show which item was clicked.

Debugging with the YUI console

Debugging is one area where JavaScript has suffered in the past—there are a range of browser plugins available which help to some extent, but if we wish to debug an issue that occurs in a browser that doesn't have these usual features, we have a problem!

YUI's answer to this problem is the YUI Console, as shown in the following image:

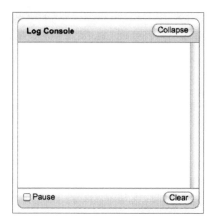

This is a widget that displays a log of all messages that have been written to the console log. These include messages from existing YUI widgets and plugins, but may also include customized messages logged from our own JavaScript code.

In this recipe, we will display the YIU console and log some example messages to it.

Getting ready

First, we create a PHP page `yui_console.php` to house the console, with the following content:

```php
<?php
  require_once(dirname(__FILE__) . '/../config.php');

  $PAGE->set_context(get_context_instance(CONTEXT_SYSTEM));
  $PAGE->set_url('/cook/yui_console.php');
  $PAGE->requires->js('/cook/yui_console.js');
```

```
    echo $OUTPUT->header();
  ?>
<h1>YUI Console</h1>
<?php
    echo $OUTPUT->footer();
  ?>
```

Next, we create the associated JavaScript file yui_console.js with the following content:

```
YUI().use("console", function(Y)
{
  var myConsole = new Y.Console();
  myConsole.render();

  Y.log("I am an info message.", "info");
  Y.log("I am a warning.", "warn");
  Y.log("I am an error.", "error");
});
```

How to do it...

Our PHP page sets up the standard Moodle programming environment we have used throughout these recipes, linking to our JavaScript file yui_console.js.

In this JavaScript file we begin by loading the console module. We now have the Y.Console object available to us. We create a new instance of this object, and then call the render method on this new instance.

Finally, we use the Y.log method to write three example log messages to demonstrate how messages are logged.

Upon loading the page in a web browser, the console is displayed, along with our three log messages as seen in the following screenshot:

How it works...

Upon loading the console module, we now have available `Y.Console` and `Y.log`.

The `Y.Console` object allows us to create a new instance of the YUI Console, and when we call its `render` method, it is displayed in the page.

Finally, we use the `Y.log` method to display messages of three different severities: Information, Warning, and Error. We can use these as we see fit to display any type of debugging information we want to render inside a normal string of text.

3

Moodle Forms Validation

In this chapter, we will cover:

- ► Adding a required field
- ► Adding a field with a maximum length
- ► Adding a field with a minimum length
- ► Adding a field length within a specified range
- ► Adding a valid e-mail address field
- ► Adding custom validation with a Regular Expression
- ► Adding a field that accepts only alphabetic characters
- ► Adding a field that accepts only alphanumeric characters
- ► Adding a field that accepts only numeric characters
- ► Rejecting punctuation characters
- ► Rejecting input without a leading zero
- ► Comparing with another field
- ► Adding a custom JavaScript validation function callback

Introduction

We often need to collect information from a user for a variety of reasons. For example, we get contact details or information about a problem they are having with our website. As is often the case, the most common solution to this problem is the use of a model from the real world: a form.

A basic web form is very similar to its paper-based counterpart, presenting a series of elements on the page where the user can enter the required information.

Web forms differ in that they give us the opportunity to ensure the quality of the information provided as it is entered. This process is known as **form validation**. Using this technique, we can apply a range of checks and constraints on the information entered. We can also ensure that all of these are satisfied before allowing the user to submit the completed form.

Moodle provides a feature-rich web forms utility based on the **PHP Extension and Application Repository** (**PEAR**) library, **QuickForm**. Forms produced in Moodle not using this library are an exception. Therefore, in this chapter we will learn how to activate the built-in JavaScript form validation functions, and also how to add our own custom JavaScript form validation logic.

The first recipe will begin by setting up a new QuickForm web form and adding a simple text field with validation. The subsequent recipes will build on this basic form and cover each of the more advanced validation options available.

Adding a required field

In this recipe, we will build a new web form using the QuickForm library, comprised of one text box field with "required field" validation applied.

This type of form validation is the simplest and most frequently used validation. It prevents the user from leaving the field blank, but imposes no further restrictions on what is actually entered.

Getting ready

First, we will prepare the form definition. Create a new file `validation_form.php` in the `cook` directory, with the following content:

```php
<?php
  require_once($CFG->libdir.'/formslib.php');
  class validation_form extends moodleform
  {
    function definition()
    {
      $mform =& $this->_form;
      $mform->addElement('text', 'mytext1', 'Required');
      $mform->addElement('submit', 'submitbutton', 'Submit');
    }
  }
?>
```

This is a very simple form definition including one text box, `mytext1`, and a submit button, `submitbutton`.

Next, prepare the form logic in this example `validation.php`, with the following content:

```php
<?php
  require_once(dirname(__FILE__) . '/../config.php');
  require_once('./validation_form.php');
  $PAGE->set_context(get_context_instance(CONTEXT_SYSTEM));
  $PAGE->set_url('/cook/validation.php');
  $PAGE->requires->js('/cook/validation.js');
  echo $OUTPUT->header();
  echo $OUTPUT->heading('Moodle JavaScript Cookbook');
  $mform = new validation_form();

  if ($fromform=$mform->get_data())
  {
    print_object($fromform);
  }
  else
  {
    $mform->display();
  }
  echo $OUTPUT->footer();
?>
```

The form logic file `validation.php` is the file that will render the form to the web browser including our validation definitions as seen in the following screenshot:

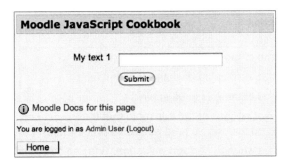

How to do it...

To add required field validation, we add the following code to our form definition in `validation_form.php` just after the field definition:

```php
$mform->addRule('mytext1', 'Required', 'required', null, 'client');
```

When we reload the `validation.php` page in a web browser and try to submit the form without entering anything into the text box, we will not be able to submit the form and will be presented with a warning explaining what we need to do to proceed as seen in the following screenshot:

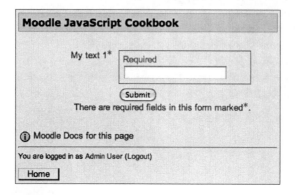

How it works...

We used the `addRule` method of `QuickForm` to define the validation requirements:

```
$mform->addRule('mytext1', 'Required', 'required', null, 'client');
```

This is controlled by the five arguments we passed to the `addRule` method:

Argument number	Description	Value
1	The name of the element to apply the rule to	`mytext1`
2	The text to be displayed when validation fails	`Required`
3	The name of the rule to be applied	`required`
4	The format options of the rule (note that the `required` rule has no options, so here we pass a `null` value)	`null`
5	Describes when to perform validation. This can be either `client` or `server`. Using `client` forces the validation to occur within the browser using JavaScript	`client`

This rule can be combined with any of the rules demonstrated in subsequent recipes. This ensures that the field is not only filled out, but in accordance with any additional constraints. Similarly, two or more of any of the rules may be combined wherever suitable.

Adding a field with a maximum length

In this recipe, we will define a field that has a maximum length constraint. This could be used when you require concise summary text to be entered, for example, when screen "real estate" is at a premium. Alternatively, it would be useful for situations when the particular column of a database into which the data will be saved only accepts a certain number of characters.

Getting ready

Please refer to the first recipe in this chapter for details on how to prepare a QuickForm web form which is the basis of this recipe.

How to do it...

Add the following code to our form definition in `validation_form.php` just after the field definition:

```
$mform->addElement('text', 'mytext2', 'Max length 5');
$mform->addRule('mytext2', 'Max length 5', 'maxlength', 5, 'client');
```

When we try out this new form element by entering six characters, we are unable to submit the form and our validation warning message is displayed as seen in the following screenshot:

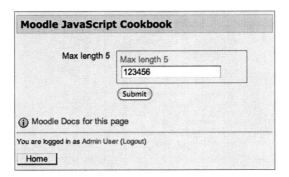

How it works...

We used the validation type `maxlength` which takes a format option in the form of an integer representing the maximum allowable length of the input.

If the user enters text comprised of more characters than we have allowed (in this example, 5), the warning message we had configured is displayed and the user is unable to submit the form until the input is made valid, that is, reduced to five or fewer characters.

Adding a field with a minimum length

In this recipe, we will apply a validation constraint which forces the user to enter text of a minimum number of characters. This could be used for cases where a certain number of characters are expected, for example, in a postal code or a telephone number.

Getting ready

Please refer to the first recipe in this chapter for details on how to prepare a QuickForm web form which is the basis of this recipe.

How to do it...

Add the following code to our form definition in `validation_form.php` just after the field definition:

```
$mform->addElement('text', 'mytext3', 'Min length 5');
$mform->addRule('mytext3', 'Min length 5', 'minlength', 5, 'client');
```

Now we can try out this new rule in the web browser. When we enter a string of only four characters, we are unable to submit the form and our warning message is displayed as seen in the following screenshot:

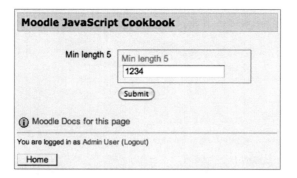

How it works...

We used the validation type `minlength` which takes a format option in the form of an integer representing the minimum allowable length of the input.

In this case, we specified that the text must contain at least five characters. When we enter a string of text of four characters or less, we are unable to submit the form until we satisfy this minimum length by providing at least five characters.

Adding a field length within in a specified range

In this recipe, we will learn how to add a rule to ensure the length of text entered falls into a specified range of numbers of characters. Again, this could be used to validate information, such as a telephone number whose length must fall in a particular range to be accepted.

Getting ready

Please refer to the first recipe in this chapter for details on how to prepare a QuickForm web form which is the basis of this recipe.

How to do it...

Add the following code to our form definition in `validation_form.php` just after the field definition:

```
$mform->addElement('text', 'mytext4', 'Length 3-5');
$mform->addRule('mytext4', 'Length 3-5', 'rangelength',
    array(3,5), 'client');
```

Now we can test this rule in a web browser and we will notice that if we enter text whose length falls outside the required range, our warning message will be displayed and the user will be unable to proceed as seen in the following screenshot:

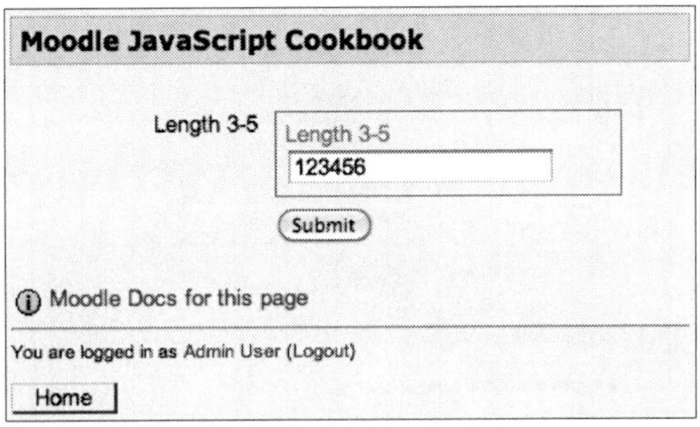

How it works...

We used the validation type, `rangelength`, which takes a format option in the form of an array containing two values: the lower and upper bounds for the length of an input. The use of an array here allows us easily to pass a pair of values in a single parameter to the `addRule` method.

Now when a user attempts to submit text of length outside the required range, our warning message will be displayed and they will be unable to submit the form until they ensure that the text meets the required validation rule.

Adding a valid e-mail address field

In this recipe, we will add a rule that ensures the user has entered a valid e-mail address. This rule should be fairly self-explanatory. It simply checks that the text is in the standard "user@ example.com" format.

Getting ready

Please refer to the first recipe in this chapter for details on how to prepare a QuickForm web form which is the basis of this recipe.

How to do it...

Add the following code to our form definition in `validation_form.php` just after the field definition:

```
$mform->addElement('text', 'mytext6', 'Email');
$mform->addRule('mytext6', 'Email', 'email', null, 'client');
```

Now we can test this rule by entering a domain name instead of a valid e-mail address. We notice that we are unable to submit the form, and our warning message is displayed as seen in the following screenshot:

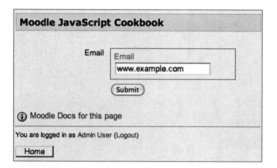

How it works...

We used the validation type `email` which requires no format option, as the format of an e-mail address is pre-defined and is therefore not configurable. If the user has entered an invalid e-mail address, our warning message will be displayed and they will be unable to submit the form until they have corrected the format of the e-mail address.

Adding custom validation with a Regular Expression

Regular Expressions are a powerful method for matching the pattern of strings of text. This has particular relevance to text validation. In this recipe, we will add a simple regular expression to validate a URL which will require the text entered to begin with `http://`. This method does, however, allow any valid Regular Expression making it particularly flexible for validating any pattern that can be represented in a Regular Expression.

Getting ready

Please refer to the first recipe in this chapter for details on how to prepare a QuickForm web form which is the basis of this recipe.

How to do it...

Add the following code to our form definition in `validation_form.php`, just after the field definition:

```
$mform->addElement('text', 'mytext5', 'URL');
$mform->addRule('mytext5', 'URL', 'regex', '^http://^', 'server');
```

When we test this new rule by entering a domain name instead of a full HTTP URL, our warning message will be displayed and once again we will not be able to submit the form until we have reformatted the text into a full HTTP URL as seen in the following screenshot:

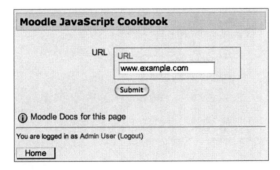

How it works...

We used the validation type `regex` which takes a format option in the form of a standard Regular Expression. In this example, the Regular Expression is a very basic form of URL validation, which simply checks to see if the input begins with `http://`.

Note that the Moodle forms API does not support client-side regular expression validation. Therefore, the fifth argument must be set to `server` as opposed to `client` in the preceding recipes.

Adding a field that accepts only alphabetic characters

In this recipe, we will add a rule that forbids all characters except alphabetic characters, that is, it allows only letters a-z in upper or lower case.

Getting ready

Please refer to the first recipe in this chapter for details on how to prepare a QuickForm web form which is the basis of this recipe.

How to do it...

Add the following code to our form definition in `validation_form.php`, just after the field definition:

```
$mform->addElement('text', 'mytext7', 'Letters only');
$mform->addRule('mytext7', 'Letters only', 'lettersonly',
  null, 'client');
```

When we test out this rule by entering numeric characters, our warning message is displayed and we are not able to submit the form as seen in the following screenshot:

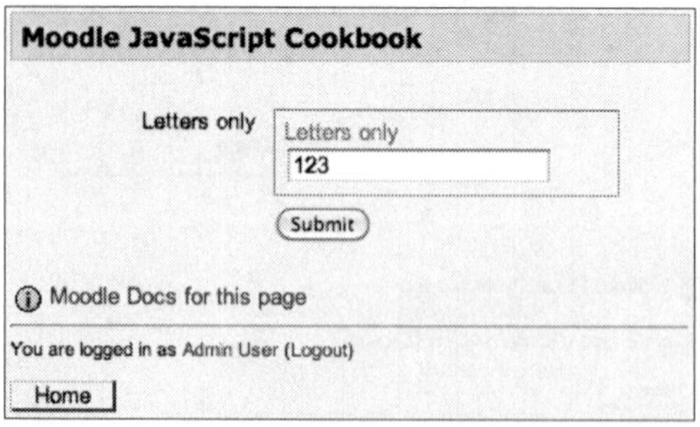

How it works...

We used the validation type `lettersonly` which does not require any format options. Now when a user attempts to submit the form after having entered any non-alphabetic characters, they will not be able to proceed but will be shown the validation warning message we had previously configured.

Adding a field that accepts only alphanumeric characters

In this recipe, we will add a rule that accepts only alphanumeric characters, that is, only the digits 0-9 and letters a-z in upper or lower case.

Getting ready

Please refer to the first recipe in this chapter for details on how to prepare a QuickForm web form which is the basis of this recipe.

How to do it...

Add the following code to our form definition in `validation_form.php`, just after the field definition:

```
$mform->addElement('text', 'mytext8', 'Alpha-numeric');
$mform->addRule('mytext8', 'Alpha-numeric', 'alphanumeric',
   null, 'client');
```

Now we can test this new rule by entering text including non-alphanumeric characters. In the following example, we have enclosed our text in non-alphanumeric double quotes. We see that the warning message is displayed and we are unable to submit the form as seen in the following screenshot:

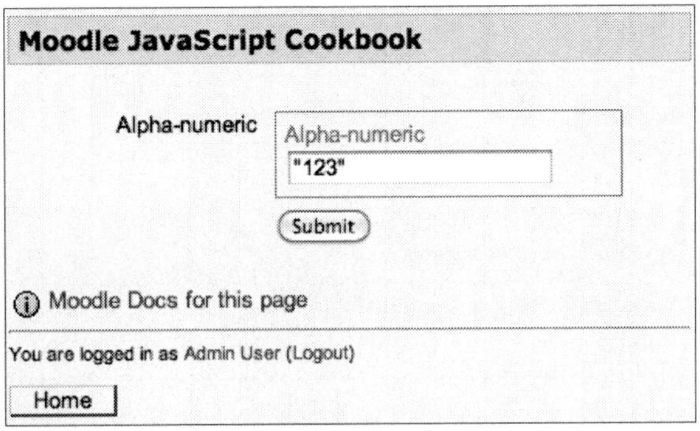

How it works...

We used the validation type `alphanumeric` which does not require any format options. When a user enters any character that is not either a digit (0-9) or a letter (a-z in either upper or lower case), a validation warning is displayed and they are unable to submit the form until they have removed the invalid characters.

Adding a field that accepts only numeric characters

In this recipe, we will add a rule that accepts only numeric characters, that is, digits 0-9. This could be useful, for example, when the user is required to enter a reference number or a currency value.

Getting ready

Please refer to the first recipe in this chapter for details on how to prepare a QuickForm web form which is the basis of this recipe.

How to do it...

Add the following code to our form definition in `validation_form.php`, just after the field definition:

```
$mform->addElement('text', 'mytext9', 'Numeric');
$mform->addRule('mytext9', 'Numeric', 'numeric', null, 'client');
```

When we test out this new rule by entering non-numeric characters (in this example, we entered the string **abc**), we see that our validation warning message is displayed and we are unable to submit the form as seen in the following screenshot:

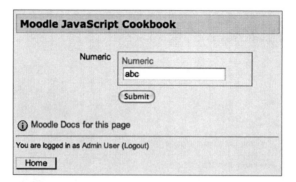

How it works...

We used the validation type `numeric` which does not require any format options. Now when a user enters anything other than the digits (0-9), they will see a validation warning message and will be unable to proceed until they have removed the invalid non-numeric characters.

Rejecting punctuation characters

In this recipe, we will add a rule that prevents the input of punctuation characters. This could be useful, for example, where you require the title of a new document to not contain periods or commas.

Getting ready

Please refer to the first recipe in this chapter for details on how to prepare a QuickForm web form which is the basis of this recipe.

How to do it...

Add the following code to our form definition in `validation_form.php`, just after the field definition:

```
$mform->addElement('text', 'mytext10', 'No punctuation');
$mform->addRule('mytext10', 'No punctuation', 'nopunctuation',
  null, 'client');
```

When we test this new rule by entering text that includes punctuation characters (a comma or period), we see that the warning message is displayed and we are unable to submit the form as seen in the following screenshot:

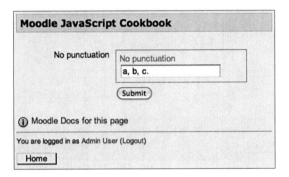

How it works...

We used the validation type `nopunctuation` which does not require any format options. When a user enters text including any punctuation character, the validation warning message will be displayed and they will be unable to submit the form until they have removed the invalid characters.

Rejecting input without a leading zero

In this recipe, we will add a rule that requires a valid number to be entered, without a leading digit, 0. This is useful for validating whole numbers without zero padding.

Getting ready

Please refer to the first recipe in this chapter for details on how to prepare a QuickForm web form which is the basis of this recipe.

How to do it...

Add the following code to our form definition in `validation_form.php`, just after the field definition:

```
$mform->addElement('text', 'mytext11', 'No leading zero');
$mform->addRule('mytext11', 'No leading zero', 'nonzero',
  null, 'client');
```

Now we can test the rule by adding an invalid sequence of digits with a leading zero: **0123**. We see that our validation warning message is displayed and we are unable to submit the form as seen in the following screenshot:

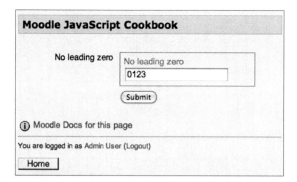

How it works...

We used the validation type `nonzero` which does not require any format options. Now when a user attempts to enter text that contains a leading zero, a validation warning message is displayed and they are unable to proceed with the form submission until the invalid character has been removed.

Comparing with another field

In this recipe, we will add a rule that allows us to ensure the contents of two fields are identical. The classic example of this type of validation is where the accuracy of the information we require from the user is vital (for example, a password or an e-mail address). We ensure that they enter it twice, compare both the entries, and display a warning if they are not identical.

Getting ready

Please refer to the first recipe in this chapter for details on how to prepare a QuickForm web form which is the basis of this recipe.

How to do it...

Add the following code to our form definition in `validation_form.php` just after the field definition:

```
$mform->addElement('text', 'mytext12', 'Must be equal (1st)');
$mform->addElement('text', 'mytext12_compare',
  'Must be equal (2nd)');
$mform->addRule( array('mytext12','mytext12_compare'),
  'Must match', 'compare', 'eq', 'server' );
```

Now we can test this new rule by entering two different values into each text box. The validation test fails due to the values not being identical, and our warning message is displayed as seen in the following screenshot:

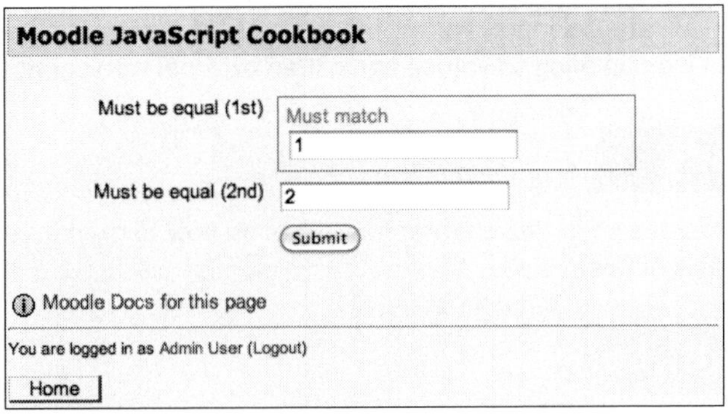

How it works...

We used the validation type `compare` which takes slightly different arguments to those previously used.

The first argument must be an array of the names of the two elements for comparison.

The format option is in the form of a string which specifies the type of comparison to apply. In this example, we used `eq` (or `==`), which specifies that the two fields must be equal. Each option has both a keyword and symbolic representation.

The following is a list of possible format options for this type:

Format option	Description
eq or ==	The first element's value is equal to the second element's value
neq or !=	The first element's value is not equal to the second element's value
gt or >	The first element's numeric value is greater than the second element's numeric value
gte or >=	The first element's numeric value is greater than or equal to the second element's numeric value
lt or <	The first element's numeric value is less than the second element's numeric value
lte or <=	The first element's numeric value is less than or equal to the second element's numeric value

Finally, the fifth argument must be set to `server` as the Moodle forms API does not support client-side comparisons.

Adding a custom JavaScript validation function callback

In this recipe, we will look at how we can validate the contents of a text box manually using JavaScript. This gives us complete flexibility by allowing us to use any tool available to us within JavaScript to validate the input. For example, we could perform validation based on today's date, or even look up allowed values against an external web service.

Getting ready

Please refer to the first recipe in this chapter for details on how to prepare a QuickForm web form which is the basis of this recipe.

How to do it...

Add the following code to our form definition in `validation_form.php`, just after the field definition:

```
$mform->addElement('text', 'mytext13', 'Custom');
$mform->addRule('mytext13', 'Custom', 'callback',
    'mycallback', 'client');
```

We specified a custom validation function `mycallback`.

In our example, we must edit `validation.php` to include a JavaScript file that includes our callback function:

```
$PAGE->requires->js('/cook/validation.js');
```

Lastly, we must add our callback function to `validation.js`:

```
function mycallback(input)
{
  if(input == 'valid')
  {
    return true;
  }
  else
  {
    return false;
  }
}
```

We simply test if the input is equal to the string `valid` or not, and return a value `true` or `false` respectively, but the function may contain any JavaScript logic necessary.

We test the rule by entering the text **invalid** and see that the validation fails and our warning message is displayed as seen in the following screenshot:

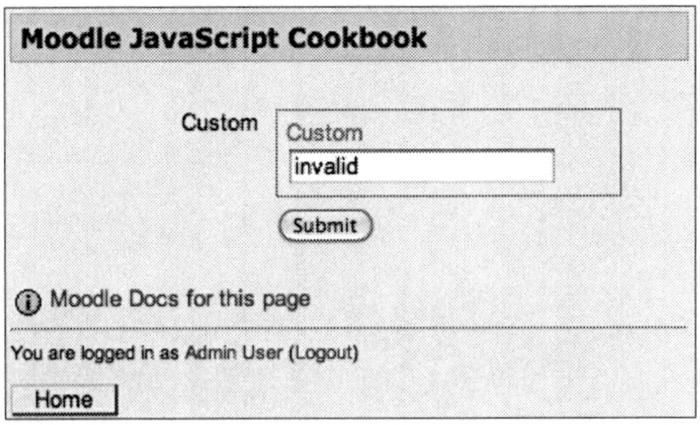

How it works...

We used the validation type `callback` which takes a format option in the form of the name of a JavaScript function.

The callback function is called by the forms API, with the value in question passed as the only parameter. The custom logic is applied to the value and the function must return either `true` or `false` as desired.

Setting the fifth argument to `client` specifies that it is a client-side callback function, and is therefore a JavaScript function. Note that setting this argument to `server` would allow the use of a PHP function for callback instead of a JavaScript function. Using an additional rule of this type would ensure that validation always occurs even if the user has disabled JavaScript in their web browser.

It is important to note that the validation techniques we covered in this chapter mostly rely on JavaScript to be enabled in the user's web browser. As a result of this, robust form validation must always be a combination of convenient client-side validation and server-side validation. This ensures that the data received will be validated regardless of what features are available within the end user's web browser. This also ensures that potentially malicious clients that attempt to circumvent client-side validation are forced to undergo additional validation that occurs on the server.

4
Manipulating Data with YUI 3

In this chapter, we will cover:

- ▶ Using IO to request a URI
- ▶ Using IO's alternative transport method for requesting external URIs
- ▶ Using PHP as a proxy to load data from an external domain
- ▶ Parsing XML with DataSource
- ▶ Parsing JSON with DataSource
- ▶ Parsing CSV data with DataSource
- ▶ Retrieving data from a Moodle 2.0 web service

Introduction

In this chapter, we will look at the ways we can use JavaScript and YUI to retrieve and display data from a range of different sources. Using these techniques, we can integrate all types of data into our Moodle applications. This list includes weather forecasts, stock updates, news feeds, any type of custom text-based data you may have from external systems, and even data from Moodle itself (both the local Moodle system and any remote systems that your code is authorized to access), retrieved via Moodle's web services API.

Moodle 2.0 includes version 3 of the Yahoo! User Interface Library (YUI 3). YUI 3 has a rich data processing API which we will look at in this chapter. We will cover how to make a simple HTTP GET request to retrieve the contents of a file using the IO module, moving on to more complex scenarios such as retrieving data from an external domain, parsing a range of data formats, and the consumption of XML-based web services.

Using IO to request a URI

In this recipe, we will use the YUI 3 module IO to retrieve the contents of a locally hosted text file. This will demonstrate how to use IO to make a simple HTTP GET request and display the response.

How to do it...

1. In this example, we will use three files:

   ❑ `text.txt`: A simple text file containing the data that we will retrieve.

   ❑ `text.php`: A PHP file that sets up the Moodle environment and defines the elements we need:

   ```php
   <?php
     require_once(dirname(__FILE__) . '/../config.php');
     $PAGE->set_context(get_context_instance(CONTEXT_SYSTEM));
     $PAGE->set_url('/cook/text.php');
     $PAGE->requires->js('/cook/text.js', true);
     echo $OUTPUT->header();
   ?>

   <form>
     <textarea id="contents"></textarea>
     <br />
     <input id="go" type="button" value="Get file contents">
   </form>

   <?php
     echo $OUTPUT->footer();
   ?>
   ```

   ❑ `text.js`: A JavaScript file that contains the actual IO request:

   ```javascript
   YUI().use('io-base', 'node', function(Y)
   {
     function success(id, o, args)
     {
       Y.one(<#contents>).set(<value>, o.responseText);
     }
     function failure(id, o, args)
     {
       Y.one(<#contents>).set(<value>, <Error: <+o.statusText);
     }
     Y.on(<io:success>, success, Y);
     Y.on(<io:failure>, failure, Y);
   ```

```
function getFile()
{
  var uri = "text.txt";
  var request = Y.io(uri);
}
Y.on(<click>, getFile, "#go");
});
```

2. In this example, we defined an input button and a `textarea` element as seen in the following screenshot:

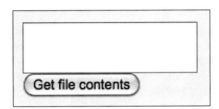

We have attached the necessary events to enable the user to display the contents of our chosen URI in the `textarea` element by clicking the **input** button.

The JavaScript file `text.js` contains the bulk of the work. First, we define a new instance of YUI 3, specifying the `io-base` module (to allow us to use IO) and the `node` module (to allow us to write into the `textarea` element).

Next, we define two callback functions (`success` and `failure`) for use with IO. We will attach these functions to the corresponding events of IO, and only one will be executed depending on the success or failure of the request.

If the request was successful, then the contents of the URI we requested are written into our text box. If the request fails, the error message will be written into the text box instead.

Finally, we defined a function `getFile` to initiate the request, and attached this to the `click` event of the **input** button.

How it works...

When the **input** button is clicked, its `click` event is fired and the `getFile` function is called.

The `getFile` function now performs a new IO request on the URI we have specified (`text.txt`).

Finally, if the request was successful, the `success` function that we attached to IO's `success` event is fired, receiving the following three arguments:

▶ **Transaction ID**: A unique identifier for the current request

- ▸ **Response object**: An object containing the response data
- ▸ **Arguments**: An array of additional arguments that may be passed when registering the callback

 Note that if the request was unsuccessful, then our `failed` function will be called with the same arguments, with the error message contained in the `statusText` property of the response object.

We have accessed the `responseText` property of the `response` object (which contains the contents of the text file we have retrieved) and displayed it within the text area `contents`.

 Due to the nature of the security restrictions of the underlying transport mechanism (`XMLHttpRequest`), it is only possible to retrieve URIs from the same domain. To retrieve data from external domains, we must either use an alternative transport mechanism, or proxy the URI through the local domain. Both approaches are detailed in subsequent recipes.

Using IO's alternative transport method for requesting external URIs

In this recipe, we will look at a method for retrieving data from an external domain. Due to security restrictions, it is not possible to make requests to an external URI with JavaScript's XMLHttpRequest. YUI avoids this restriction by including a built-in alternative transport mechanism based on Adobe Flash. In this way, any trusted domain with a valid cross-domain policy file may be used as a source of data.

Getting ready

First, we need to ensure that the remote domain is configured to accept incoming client requests. This is done by installing a cross-domain policy file `crossdomain.xml` on the remote domain. This cross-domain policy file specifies which domains are authorized to make requests via Adobe Flash (`.swf`) applications.

The following example configures the domain `remote.example.com` to accept incoming HTTP requests from any host on `example.com`.

Contents of the `http://remote.example.com/crossdomain.xml` file are as follows:

```
<?xml version="1.0"?>
<!DOCTYPE cross-domain-policy SYSTEM
"http://www.adobe.com/xml/dtds/cross-domain-policy.dtd">
<cross-domain-policy>
  <allow-access-from domain="*.example.com "/>
```

```
<allow-http-request-headers-from domain=
  "*.example.com" headers="*"/>
</cross-domain-policy>
```

How to do it...

1. In this example, we will retrieve the contents of a text file from the remote server at `http://remote.example.com/text.txt`.

2. We will now set up the PHP and JavaScript files necessary for this recipe:

    ❑   `text_external.php`: A PHP file that sets up the Moodle environment and defines the elements we need:

    ```php
    <?php
      require_once(dirname(__FILE__) . '/../config.php');
      $PAGE->set_context(get_context_instance(CONTEXT_SYSTEM));
      $PAGE->set_url('/cook/text_external.php');
      $PAGE->requires->js('/cook/text_external.js');
      echo $OUTPUT->header();
    ?>

    <form>
      <textarea id="contents»></textarea>
      <br />
      <input id="go" type="button"
        value="Get file contents" disabled="disabled">
    </form>

    <?php
      echo $OUTPUT->footer();
    ?>
    ```

    ❑   `text_external.js`: The accompanying JavaScript file that executes the request:

    ```javascript
    YUI().use('io-xdr', 'node', function(Y)
    {
      var xdrConfig =
      {
        src:'../lib/yui/3.2.0/build/io/io.swf'
      };
      Y.io.transport(xdrConfig);
      var cfg =
      {
        xdr: { use: ‹flash› },
        on:
        {
          success: completed,
    ```

```
          failure: failed
        }
      };
      function completed(id, o, args)
      {
        Y.one('#contents').set('value', o.responseText);
      }
      function failed(id, o, args)
      {
        Y.one('#contents').set(value, 'Error: '+args);
      }
      var getFile = function()
      {
        var uri = "http://example.com/text.txt";
        var request = Y.io(uri, cfg);
      }
      var ready = function()
      {
        Y.one('#go').set("disabled", false);
        Y.on('click', getFile, "#go");
      }
      Y.on('io:xdrReady', ready, Y);
    });
```

3. The content of `text_external.php` is similar to that used in the previous recipe with the exception that the **input** button has been disabled so that it will only be usable when the request transport mechanism is ready for use. Here, we have defined a simple form with a text area for displaying the response text, and an input button to allow the user to initiate the request as seen in the following screenshot:

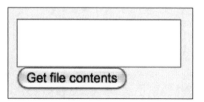

4. The file `text_external.js` is where the request is made. First, we create a new instance of YUI 3, loading the modules `io-xdr` (for cross-domain request transport) and `node` (for manipulating the DOM elements).

5. Next, we specify the path to IO's XDR transport proxy Flash file (this is relative to the path of the final HTML output) and apply this configuration to the IO transport object.

6. Next, we define another configuration object for the main IO object that specifies we will use the "flash" transport mechanism, and also subscribes to the `success` event.

7. We now define a function to execute the request, which will later be attached to the input button's `click` event.

8. Finally, we define and register a callback function for IO's `xdrReady` event.

How it works...

When the page loads, our JavaScript code initializes the cross-domain request (XDR) functionality of IO and the relevant events are subscribed to. The Flash movie is loaded into the page and when it is ready for use the `xdrReady` event is fired.

We have subscribed to the `xdrReady` event and when this is fired, we enable the **input** button and attach a function to the `click` event that performs the actual request.

When the request completes successfully, the `success` event is fired and calls our function that retrieves the response body text and displays it in the `textarea` element on our PHP page. Alternatively, if the request fails, our `failed` event handler is fired and the error message is displayed in the text box.

Using PHP as a proxy to load data from an external domain

If you wish to retrieve data from a trusted external source that does not have a valid cross-domain policy file installed, then you can use a local PHP file as a proxy to download the file for you.

This method has the disadvantage that the overhead of retrieving the file is moved to the server rather than the client as in the previous YUI method. However, it may need to be used as a last resort when it is not feasible to install a cross-domain policy file on the remote domain.

How to do it...

1. This example uses one PHP file, `get_external_data.php`:

```php
<?php
    require_once('../config.php');
    require_once('../lib/filelib.php');
    $uri = 'http://remote.example.com/text.txt';
    echo download_file_content($uri);
?>
```

2. First, we set up the basic Moodle environment by including the global `config.php` file.

3. Next, we include Moodle's file API library which provides the function `download_file_content`.

4. We now define the URI of the file we wish to download, and output the result of `download_file_content`.

5. Finally, we may use this new PHP file as a data source in place of the original external URI.

How it works...

Moodle's file API provides the `download_file_content` function, which returns the contents of the supplied URI.

As this file is hosted on the local domain, JavaScript interacts with this data as if it were a local file, avoiding the security issues that occur when loading data from remote domains.

Parsing XML with DataSource

Many websites and web services make data available in XML format (as RSS, for example). In this recipe, will load an XML file, parse the contents, and display it within a text box.

How to do it...

1. In this example, we will use the following three files:

   ❑ `data.xml`: A very simple example XML data file with the following contents:

   ```xml
   <?xml version="1.0" encoding="UTF-8" ?>
   <list>
     <item>Item One</item>
     <item>Item Two</item>
     <item>Item Three</item>
     <item>Item Four</item>
     <item>Item Five</item>
     <item>Item Six</item>
     <item>Item Seven</item>
     <item>Item Eight</item>
     <item>Item Nine</item>
     <item>Item Ten</item>
   </list>
   ```

   ❑ `datasource_xml.php`: A PHP page with an input button for initiating the request and a text area to display the results:

   ```php
   <?php
     require_once(dirname(__FILE__) . '/../config.php');
   ```

```php
    $PAGE->set_context(get_context_instance(CONTEXT_SYSTEM));
    $PAGE->set_url('/cook/datasource_xml.php');
    $PAGE->requires->js('/cook/datasource_xml.js');
    echo $OUTPUT->header();
?>

<form>
  <textarea id="contents" rows="10"></textarea>
  <br />
  <input id="go" type="button" value="Get XML">
</form>

<?php
  echo $OUTPUT->footer();
?>
```

❑ `datasource_xml.js`: The accompanying JavaScript file containing the YUI data logic:

```javascript
YUI().use('datasource-io', 'datasource-xmlschema', 'node',
  function(Y) {
  var dataSource = new Y.DataSource.IO({source:"./data.
  xml"});

  dataSource.plug(Y.Plugin.DataSourceXMLSchema, {
    schema: {
      resultListLocator: "item",
      resultFields: [{key:"text", locator:"."}]
    }
  });

  function loadXML(){
    dataSource.sendRequest({
      callback: {
        success: function(e){
          var xmlData = "";
          Y.Array.each(e.response.results, function(item)
            {xmlData += item.text + '\n'});
          document.getElementById('contents').value =
          xmlData;
        },
        failure: function(e){
        alert(e.error.message);
        }
      }
    });
  }
  Y.on('click', loadXML, "#go");
});
```

2. First, we set up a now-familiar PHP page linking to our accompanying JavaScript file. We include some basic form elements such as a text area to display the data we have retrieved, and an input button to which we shall attach an event that runs our JavaScript.

3. Moving on to our JavaScript file, we begin by creating a new instance of YUI and loading in the modules we require:

Module	Purpose
`datasource-io`	Data retrieval
`datasource-xmlschema`	Data parsing
`node`	DOM access (for displaying data in page)

4. First, we define a new instance of `DataSource.IO`, passing the path to our data file.

5. Next, we tell the data source to use the `DataSourceXMLSchema` plug-in, so we can efficiently parse our XML data into an easy-to-use native JavaScript object.

6. Next, we define a function `loadXML` that performs the loading and parsing of the data. We call the `sendRequest` method of the data source, and define two callback functions: `success` and `failure`.

7. For the `success` callback function, we simply iterate the contents of the response results to build a string which is then displayed in the page's textarea element.

8. The `failure` callback function simply displays the message of the error that occurred, all being well we will not see this!

9. Finally, we attach the `loadXML` function to our input button to allow the user to initiate the request.

How it works...

When the page is loaded, a new `DataSource.IO` object is instantiated with the source set to the data file that we wish to retrieve. Additionally, the object is configured to use `DataSourceXMLSchema` that describes the format of the file and allows it to automatically be parsed into a format useful to us.

When the user clicks the **input** button, the `click` event is fired and our attached function is called. This function performs the request to retrieve the data, and if everything is successful, the `success` callback function is run.

This callback function is passed the response results, which is an object generated from our XML, in the format defined by the `XMLSchema` definition we supplied. In this example, we used the `Array.each` utility to build a string containing a list of the results separated by line breaks, which we finally display in the `textarea` element.

Parsing JSON with DataSource

In this recipe, we will use DataSource in conjunction with the `JSONSchema` plug-in to retrieve and parse a data file in the JSON format.

Getting ready

We will use three files in this example:

- `data.json`: A data file in JSON format with the following contents:

```
{
  "list":[
    {"name":"Item One"},
    {"name":"Item Two"},
    {"name":"Item Three"},
    {"name":"Item Four"},
    {"name":"Item Five"},
    {"name":"Item Six"},
    {"name":"Item Seven"},
    {"name":"Item Eight"},
    {"name":"Item Nine"},
    {"name":"Item Ten"}
    ]
}
```

- `datasource_json.php`: A PHP page with an input button for initiating the request and a `textarea` to display the results:

```php
<?php
  require_once(dirname(__FILE__) . '/../config.php');
  $PAGE->set_url('/cook/datasource_json.php');
  $PAGE->requires->js('/cook/datasource_json.js');
  echo $OUTPUT->header();
?>

<form>
  <textarea id="contents" rows="10"></textarea>
  <br />
  <input id="go" type="button" value="Get JSON">
</form>

<?
  echo $OUTPUT->footer();
?>
```

▶ `datasource_json.js`: The accompanying JavaScript file containing the YUI data logic:

```
YUI().use('datasource-io', 'datasource-jsonschema', 'node',
  function(Y) {
    var dataSource = new Y.DataSource.IO({source:"./data.json"});
    dataSource.plug(Y.Plugin.DataSourceJSONSchema, {
      schema: {
        resultListLocator: "list",
        resultFields: ["name"]
      }
    });

    function loadJSON(){
    dataSource.sendRequest({
      callback: {
        success: function(e){
          var jsonData = "";
          Y.Array.each(e.response.results, function(item)
          {
            jsonData += item.name + ‹\n›
          });
          document.getElementById(‹contents›).value = jsonData;
        },
        failure: function(e){
          alert(e.error.message);
        }
      }
    });
  }
  Y.on('click', loadJSON, "#go");
});
```

How to do it...

1. First we set up a now-familiar PHP page linking to our accompanying JavaScript file. We include some basic form elements such as a `textarea` to display the data we have retrieved and an **input** button on which we will attach an event that runs our JavaScript.

2. Moving on to our JavaScript file, we begin by creating a new instance of YUI and loading in the modules we require:

Module	Purpose
datasource-io	Data retrieval
datasource-jsonschema	Data parsing
node	DOM access (for displaying data in page)

3. First, we define a new instance of DataSource.IO, passing the path to our data file.

4. Next, we tell the data source to use the DataSourceJSONSchema plug-in so that we can efficiently parse our JSON data into our desired format.

5. Next, we define a function loadJSON that performs the loading and parsing of the data. We call the sendRequest method of the data source, and define two callback functions: success and failure.

6. For the success callback function, we simply iterate the contents of the response results to build a string which we then display in the page's textarea element.

7. The failure callback function simply displays the message of the error that occurred. If all is well, we will not see this!

8. Finally, we attach the loadJSON function to our **input** button to allow the user to initiate the request.

How it works...

When the page is loaded, a new DataSource.IO object is instantiated with the source set to the data file that we wish to retrieve. Additionally, the object is configured to use DataSourceJSONSchema that describes the format of the file and allows it to be automatically parsed into a format useful to us.

When the user clicks the **input** button, the click event is fired and our attached function is called. This function performs the request to retrieve the data, and if everything is successful, the success callback function runs.

This callback function is passed the response result, which is an object generated from our JSON data, in the format defined by the JSONSchema definition we supplied. In this example, we used the Array.each utility to build a string containing a list of the results, separated by line breaks, which we finally display in the textarea element.

Parsing CSV data with DataSource

In this recipe, we will parse a simple two-column CSV data file using DataSource and the TextSchema plug-ins.

Getting ready

We will again require three files:

- `data.csv`: A two-column CSV data file that we will use as our data source:

  ```
  1,Item One
  2,Item Two
  3,Item Three
  4,Item Four
  5,Item Five
  6,Item Six
  7,Item Seven
  8,Item Eight
  9,Item Nine
  10,Item Ten
  ```

- `datasource_csv.php`: A PHP page with an **input** button for initiating the request and a `textarea` to display the results:

  ```php
  <?php
    require_once(dirname(__FILE__) . '/../config.php');
    $PAGE->set_url('/cook/datasource_json.php');
    $PAGE->requires->js('/cook/datasource_csv.js');
    echo $OUTPUT->header();
  ?>

  <form>
    <textarea id="contents" rows="10"></textarea>
    <br />
    <input id="go" type="button" value="Get CSV">
  </form>

  <?
    echo $OUTPUT->footer();
  ?>
  ```

- `datasource_csv.js`: The accompanying JavaScript file containing the YUI data logic:

  ```javascript
  YUI().use('datasource-io', 'datasource-textschema', 'node',
    function(Y) {
      var dataSource = new Y.DataSource.IO({source:"./data.csv"});
      dataSource.plug(Y.Plugin.DataSourceTextSchema, {
        schema: {
          resultDelimiter: "\n",
          fieldDelimiter: ",",
          resultFields: ["id","name"]
        }
  ```

```
    });
    function loadCSV(){
      dataSource.sendRequest({
        callback: {
          success: function(e){
            var csvData = "";
            Y.Array.each(e.response.results, function(item)
            {
              csvData += item.id + ": " + item.name + '\n'
            });
            document.getElementById('contents').value = csvData;
          },
          failure: function(e){
            alert(e.error.message);
          }
        }
      });
    }
  Y.on(<click>, loadCSV, "#go");
});
```

How to do it...

1. First, we set up a now-familiar PHP page linking to our accompanying JavaScript file. We include some basic form elements such as a text area to display the data we have retrieved, and an **input** button on which we shall attach an event that runs our JavaScript.

2. Moving on to our JavaScript file, we begin by creating a new instance of YUI and loading in the modules we require:

Module	Purpose
`datasource-io`	Data retrieval
`datasource-textschema`	Data parsing
`node`	DOM access (for displaying data in page)

3. First, we define a new instance of DataSource.IO, passing the path to our data file.

4. Next, we tell the data source to use the `DataSourceTextSchema` plug-in so we can efficiently parse our CSV data into a native JavaScript object.

5. Next, we define a function `loadCSV` that performs the loading and parsing of the data. We call the `sendRequest` method of the data source, and define two callback functions: `success` and `failure`.

6. For the `success` callback function, we simply iterate the contents of the response results to build a string, which we then display in the page's `textarea` element.

7. The `failure` callback function simply displays the message of the error that occurred. If everything is well, we will not see this!

8. Finally, we attach the `loadCSV` function to our **input** button to allow the user to initiate the request.

How it works...

When the page is loaded, a new `DataSource.IO` object is instantiated with the source set to the data file that we wish to retrieve. Additionally, the object is configured to use a `DataSourceTextSchema` that describes the format of the file and allows it to be automatically parsed into a native JavaScript object.

When the user clicks the **input** button, the `click` event is fired and our attached function is called. This function performs the request to retrieve the data, and if everything is successful, the `success` callback function runs.

This callback function is passed the response result, which is an object generated from our CSV data in the format defined by the `TextSchema` definition we supplied. In this example, we used the `Array.each` utility to build a string containing a list of the results, separated by line breaks, which we finally display in the `textarea` element.

Retrieving data from a Moodle 2.0 web service

New in Moodle 2.0 is a plug-in-based web service layer supporting various web service standards. In this recipe, we will use Moodle 2.0's built-in REST web service to retrieve a list of groups on a specific course and display this list in a text box on our page.

Getting ready

Enable web services in your Moodle 2.0 installation, and configure the REST protocol for use. Make a note of the security token that is defined as part of this process as we will require it later on. Refer to the Moodle documentation wiki for further details on how to enable web services at `http://docs.moodle.org/en/Web_Services`.

How to do it...

1. First, we create a basic PHP page to set up the Moodle programming environment which includes a text box and an **input** button that we will use to retrieve and display the web service data. This file, `datasource_moodlews.php` will have the following

content:

```php
<?php
  require_once(dirname(__FILE__) . '/../config.php');
  $PAGE->set_context(get_context_instance(CONTEXT_SYSTEM));
  $PAGE->set_url('/cook/datasource_moodlews.php');
  $PAGE->requires->js('/cook/datasource_moodlews.js');
  echo $OUTPUT->header();
?>

<form>
  <textarea id="contents" rows="10"></textarea>
  <br />
  <input id="go" type="button" value="Get Data">
</form>

<?php
  echo $OUTPUT->footer();
?>
```

2. This file references an accompanying JavaScript file `datasource_moodlews.js`. This is where the code that communicates with the web service will be stored, and has the following content:

```javascript
YUI().use('datasource-io', 'datasource-xmlschema', 'node',
  function(Y) {
    var token = "cbbf322ae646cde4aa0e72f69cafc077";
    var wsFunction = "moodle_group_get_course_groups";
    var uri = "../webservice/rest/server.php?wstoken=
      "+token+"&wsfunction="+wsFunction;
    var dataSource = new Y.DataSource.IO({source:uri});
    dataSource.plug(Y.Plugin.DataSourceXMLSchema,
    {
      schema:
      {
        resultListLocator: "SINGLE",
        resultFields: [{key:"name",
          locator:"KEY[@name='name']/VALUE"}]
      }
    });

    function loadXML()
    {
      dataSource.sendRequest
      ({
        request:"courseid=2",
        cfg:
        {
```

```
                    method:"post",
                    headers:
                    {
                      'Content-Type': 'application/x-www-form-urlencoded'
                    }
                },
                callback:
                {
                  success: function(e)
                  {
                    var xmlData = "";
                    Y.Array.each
                    (
                      e.response.results,
                      function(item)
                      {
                        xmlData += item.name + <\n>
                      }
                    );
                    Y.one('#contents').set('value', xmlData);
                  },
                  failure: function(e)
                  {
                    alert(e.error.message);
                  }
                }
              });
          }
          Y.on(<click>, loadXML, "#go");
        });
```

3. The file `datasource_moodlews.php` is based on our usual template for a Moodle PHP file, and includes just two additional elements—a text box (text area) and an input button as seen in the following screenshot:

4. Later in our JavaScript, we will attach a `click` event to this button that retrieves the data we require from the web service and then displays it in the textbox.

5. Moving on to the JavaScript file `datasource_moodlews.js`, this is where we will do the bulk of the work involved in retrieving and displaying the data. We begin by loading the necessary YUI modules:

Module	Purpose
`datasource-io`	Making the call to retrieve data from the web service
`datasource-xmlschema`	Parsing the XML response data
`node`	Manipulating DOM elements (attaching events, setting text values)

6. Define two variables for use in the web service query, starting with the security token. This is the token that was set up within Moodle at the start of the recipe. Next is the name of the web service function we wish to call, `moodle_group_get_course_groups`.

7. Use these two variables to build the URI of the web service method we will call and create a new `DataSource.IO` object base on that URI.

8. Define how `DataSource.IO` will return the data to us by plugging in the `DataSourceXMLSchema` plug-in and providing it with a schema that describes the format of the XML that is returned from the Moodle web service.

9. Define a function `loadXML` that will perform the request. This is done using the `sendRequest` method of the `DataSource.IO` object. This takes one parameter in the form of an object containing the following three objects:

    ❑   `request`: this object is a string that defines the list of name-value pairs that are used as input to the web service method. In this case, we have only course ID with a value of `2`.

    ❑   `cfg`: this object is where we define the HTTP method of the request (POST). It also allows us to set additional HTTP headers for use in the request. We set the `Content-Type` header to `application/x-www-form-url-encoded` to ensure our name-value pairs are encoded correctly.

    ❑   `callback`: this object consists of two objects: `success` and `failure`. These objects are functions, with only one being called which corresponds to the success or failure of the request. In our `success` function, we parse the data that was returned and write it into our text box. The `failure` function displays an alert with the error message that was given by `DataSource.IO`.

10. Finally, we attach the `loadXML` function to our button's `click` event.

11. Now, when we test this code in a browser, we click the **Get Data** button and see that the list of groups is returned as seen in the following screenshot:

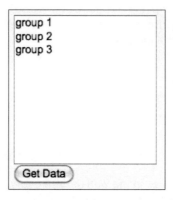

12. This matches the list of groups that we see if we check the group administration page for that course within Moodle itself as seen in the following screenshot:

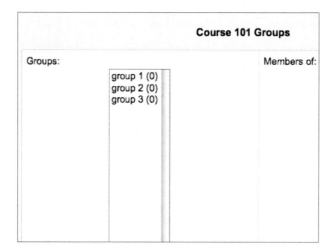

How it works...

When the page is loaded, a new `DataSource.IO` object is instantiated which was configured with the URI of our web service method and includes the necessary security token. This object is also configured with the `DataSourceXMLSchema` plug-in, which describes how the data that is returned should be parsed and presented to our callback function.

When the user clicks the **input** button, the `click` event is fired and our attached function is called. This function performs the request to retrieve the data, and if everything is successful, the `success` callback function is run.

This callback function is passed the response result in the form of a native JavaScript object `e.response.results` which corresponds to the format that we defined in the `DataSourceXMLSchema` plug-in schema. We then used the `Array.each` utility to build a string containing a list of the results, separated by line breaks, which we finally display in the `textarea` element.

5
Working with Data Tables

In this chapter, we will cover:

- ▸ Initializing a YUI DataSource
- ▸ Displaying data
- ▸ Basic column sorting
- ▸ Adding paging
- ▸ Enabling scrolling
- ▸ Enabling editing

Introduction

Database driven applications, such as Moodle, require efficient methods of displaying data to users (for example, a table of assignment grades or other recent user activity). This typically takes the form of an HTML table, the familiar grid of columns and rows in the style of a spreadsheet. Though generated dynamically from a database on the server, by the time these tables are rendered to the browser they are fairly static, representing a non-interactive grid of data on screen.

There is a lot of scope within JavaScript (and the YUI) for us to bring these static tables to life by enabling functionality more reminiscent of a spreadsheet application than a basic web page. Examples of this functionality include the following:

- ▸ **Sorting**: The ability to sort columns alphabetically or numerically in ascending or descending order.

- ▸ **Paging**: The ability to click through smaller "chunks" of the contents of the table by splitting it up into pages of a certain size. This is a great way to handle scenarios where there may be a large number of records in the table and it would be impractical to display them all on the screen simultaneously.

- ▸ **Scrolling**: An alternative to paging for managing long lists of records that otherwise would be too cumbersome to display in one list.

- ▸ **In-line editing**: Allowing users to make quick updates to values in the table from the same interface that the user uses to view the data.

YUI 2 includes a very powerful DataTable control which implements these features. This will be the focus of this chapter. We will start with a basic static HTML table of data and gradually enhance it with JavaScript and the YUI to implement the functionality described, in line with the best practice of progressive enhancement.

The reason we are using a YUI 2 control here instead of a YUI 3 control is that, at the time of writing, there is no suitable counterpart control in YUI 3. However, we can easily load and use YUI 2 controls within the new YUI 3 framework, allowing us access to the best features of both YUI 2 and 3.

Initializing a YUI DataSource

In this recipe, we will create a static HTML table of data in the classic way. Once we have created this table, we will go on to use it as the basis for a data source object that we can in turn pass to the YUI DataTable object.

The DataTable control can be created based on any valid `YAHOO.util.DataSource`. In keeping with the spirit of the concept of progressive enhancement, in this example we will use an HTML table as the data source. This allows browsers without JavaScript to view a standard HTML table of the data, while browsers with JavaScript enabled can take advantage of these enhancements.

How to do it...

We begin by creating a PHP file (`datatable.php`) in the `cook` directory. This sets up a basic Moodle environment and then displays our data in an HTML table:

```php
<?php
require_once(dirname(__FILE__) . '/../config.php');

$PAGE->set_context(get_context_instance(CONTEXT_SYSTEM));
$PAGE->set_url('/cook/datatable.php');
$PAGE->requires->js('/cook/datatable.js', true);

echo $OUTPUT->header();
```

```
?>
<div id="container">
  <table id="cooktable">
      <thead>
          <tr>
              <th>Chapter No.</th>
              <th>Title</th>
          </tr>
      </thead>
      <tbody>
          <tr>
              <td>1</td>
              <td>Combining Moodle and JavaScript</td>
          </tr>
          <tr>
              <td>2</td>
              <td>Moodle and Yahoo! User Interface Library (YUI)</td>
          </tr>
          <tr>
              <td>3</td>
              <td>Moodle forms validation</td>
          </tr>
          <tr>
              <td>4</td>
              <td>Manipulating data</td>
          </tr>
          <tr>
              <td>5</td>
              <td>Working with data tables</td>
          </tr>
          <tr>
              <td>6</td>
              <td>Enhancing page elements</td>
          </tr>
          <tr>
              <td>7</td>
              <td>Advanced layout techniques</td>
          </tr>
          <tr>
              <td>8</td>
              <td>Animating components</td>
          </tr>
          <tr>
              <td>9</td>
```

```
            <td>Integrating external libraries</td>
          </tr>
        </tbody>
    </table>
</div>
<?php
echo $OUTPUT->footer();

?>
```

This page produces the layout, as shown in the following screenshot:

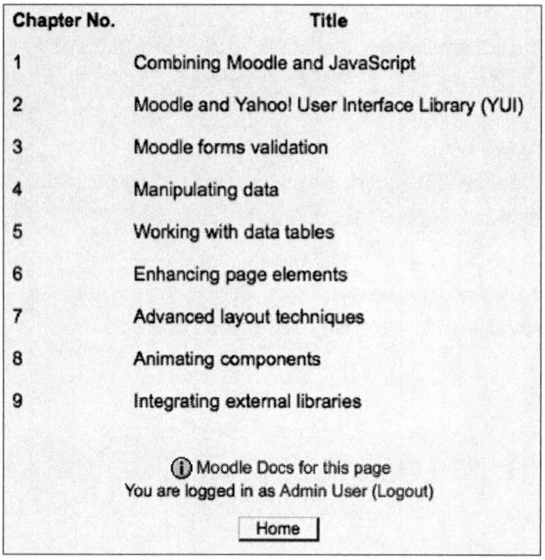

Chapter No.	Title
1	Combining Moodle and JavaScript
2	Moodle and Yahoo! User Interface Library (YUI)
3	Moodle forms validation
4	Manipulating data
5	Working with data tables
6	Enhancing page elements
7	Advanced layout techniques
8	Animating components
9	Integrating external libraries

ⓘ Moodle Docs for this page
You are logged in as Admin User (Logout)

Home

Next, we add the necessary code to our associated JavaScript file (datatable.js):

```
YUI().use("yui2-datatable", function(Y) {

    var YAHOO = Y.YUI2;

    var dataSource = new YAHOO.util.DataSource(YAHOO.util.Dom.
      get("cooktable"));
        dataSource.responseType = YAHOO.util.DataSource.TYPE_HTMLTABLE;

        dataSource.responseSchema = {
            fields: [
                { key: "chapter", parser: "number" },
                { key: "title", parser: "string" }
            ]
        };
}
```

The HTML table we have constructed consists of a standard two-column table with headers and rows clearly defined in their respective tags. Verifying that the table header information is stored correctly inside `<thead>` and `<th>` tags allows YUI 2 to ensure that it is not included as part of the actual data set.

Moving on to our JavaScript code, we initialize a new YUI 3 environment in the standard way, loading the required module: `yui2-datatable`.

There is currently no native YUI 3 version of the DataTable object, so we will use the YUI 2 version. This is done by setting up the YUI 2 object `YAHOO` which is available in the object `Y.YUI2`

Next, we create a new YUI 2 DataSource, passing in a reference to our HTML table with ID `cooktable`. We then set the `responseType` of the DataTable to identify it as an HTML table.

Finally, we set the `responseSchema` of the DataTable to identify each column with a key and also define the data type of the columns; in this case, `number` and `string` respectively.

We now have a YUI 2 DataSource object populated from our HTML table. This can be used with any YUI 2 DataSource compatible code. In this example, we will be passing this object to the DataTable control to as the basis for an interactive data table control.

How it works...

We used a mixture of YUI 2 and YUI 3 code. YUI 3 allows us to use the simplified syntax for loading modules, and YUI 2 allows us to use the DataTable control in lieu of a YUI 3 replacement.

YUI 3 provides us with an instance of YUI 2, which is available in 'Y.YUI2'. We copied this object into the `YAHOO` object, for the convenience of being able to use exactly the same syntax as in native YUI 2 code.

When we point the DataSource constructor at our HTML table, it is able to extract the data into a native YUI 2 DataSource object by using the responseType `YAHOO.util.DataSource.TYPE_HTMLTABLE`.

Displaying data

In this recipe, we will use the DataSource object that we prepared from our HTML table in the previous recipe. We will use it as the basis for a new DataTable control, and we will begin to see the enhancements that this control affords.

We now have a DataSource object available, we can move on to creating the actual DataTable control. This example builds on the previous recipe, adding additional code to the existing JavaScript. However, it should be clear that the DataSource we built in the previous recipe may be substituted for any other (for example, a DataSource built from data retrieved from an XML web service).

How to do it...

Open the `datatable.js` file from our previous recipe, and add the DataTable definition code as highlighted, after the data source has been defined. The file contents should then match the following:

```
YUI().use("yui2-datatable", "yui2-paginator", function(Y) {

    var YAHOO = Y.YUI2;

    var dataSource = new YAHOO.util.DataSource(YAHOO.util.Dom.
      get("cooktable"));
        dataSource.responseType = YAHOO.util.DataSource.TYPE_HTMLTABLE;

        dataSource.responseSchema = {
            fields: [
                { key: "chapter", parser: "number" },
                { key: "title", parser: "string" }
            ]
        };

    var columns = [
        {
            key: "chapter",
            label: "Chapter No.",
            formatter: "number"
        },
        {
            key: "title",
            label: "Title",
            formatter: "string"
        }
    ];

    var dataTable = new YAHOO.widget.DataTable
      ("container", columns, dataSource);

});
```

We first create a definition of the columns in the DataTable by creating an array of objects containing the following properties:

Property	Description
key	A key name for the column
label	A text label for the column (displayed in the column header)
formatter	The type of the data in the column, used for formatting

We then create a new YUI 2 DataTable object, which takes the following three arguments:

1. The ID of a DOM object to use as a container for the data source

2. The column definition array created earlier

3. The DataSource object from which to populate the table

How it works...

The DataTable constructor uses the information we provided to generate a YUI 2 DataTable object, which is inserted into the containing object we have specified, and populates it with data from our DataSource, consistent with the schema information we supplied in the column definition array.

We may now execute the page and see our standard HTML table transformed, as shown in the following screenshot:

Chapter No.	Title
1	Combining Moodle and JavaScript
2	Moodle and Yahoo! User Interface Library (YUI)
3	Moodle forms validation
4	Manipulating data
5	Working with data tables
6	Enhancing page elements
7	Advanced layout techniques
8	Animating components
9	Integrating external libraries

Basic column sorting

In this recipe, we will enable column sorting. This will allow the user to click on the header cells of the table to sort the entire table alphabetically or numerically by the contents of that column. Clicking once will sort ascending, and clicking a second time will sort descending. Subsequent clicks will toggle between these two states.

Getting ready

Open the `datatable.js` file for editing. We will modify the column definitions to allow sorting.

How to do it...

Modify the column definition as follows:

```
var columns = [
    {
        key: "chapter",
        label: "Chapter No.",
        formatter: "number",
        sortable: true
    {
        key: "title",
        label: "Title",
        formatter: "string",
        sortable: true
    }
];
```

How it works...

We simply added an extra property to each column definition object: `sortable`.

Setting this to `true` activates the built-in column sorting functionality for each column that we have enabled.

The following screenshot shows that the DataTable has been sorted alphabetically on the **Title** column, simply by clicking on the column header:

Chapter No.	Title
7	Advanced layout techniques
8	Animating components
1	Combining Moodle and JavaScript
6	Enhancing page elements
9	Integrating external libraries
4	Manipulating data
2	Moodle and Yahoo! User Interface Library (YUI)
3	Moodle forms validation
5	Working with data tables

Similarly, we may sort the rows of the table by chapter number, in descending numerical order by clicking on the **Chapter No.** column header, once to sort it in ascending order, and twice for descending order, as shown in the following screenshot:

Chapter No. ▾	Title
9	Integrating external libraries
8	Animating components
7	Advanced layout techniques
6	Enhancing page elements
5	Working with data tables
4	Manipulating data
3	Moodle forms validation
2	Moodle and Yahoo! User Interface Library (YUI)
1	Combining Moodle and JavaScript

Adding paging

In this recipe, we will enable data paging. We will implement the YUI Paginator control, and configure the DataTable to display rows in blocks of five records. The YUI 2 DataTable control is compatible with the Paginator control. This allows us to enable familiar paging controls for our DataTable, which is particularly useful for large data sets.

Getting ready

Open the `datatable.js` file for editing. We will add an extra configuration object to add to the DataTable constructor.

How to do it...

First, we must include an additional module: `yui2-paginator`. We do this by modifying the first line of our code as follows:

```
YUI().use("yui2-datatable", "yui2-paginator", function(Y) {
```

Below the column definition object, add the following code:

```
var config = {
    paginator : new YAHOO.widget.Paginator({
      rowsPerPage: 5
      }),
};
```

Next, we must pass this new configuration object to the DataTable by passing it as the fourth argument to the constructor. Modify the definition of the variable `dataTable` to match the following code:

```
var dataTable = new YAHOO.widget.DataTable("container", columns,
dataSource, config);
```

How it works...

The DataTable allows us to pass a configuration object as the fourth argument.

One property of this is the `paginator` property, which we set to a new instance of the Paginator control (with a page size of 5).

The DataTable has applied our configuration and added the Paginator control. We can now use the page links it has generated to skip through the list page by page as seen in the following screenshots:

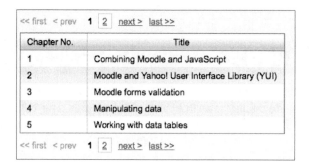

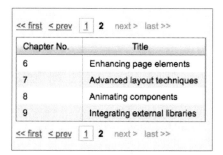

Enabling scrolling

In this recipe, we will implement a scrolling data table, an alternative method to paging that allows us to better handle the display of large data sets which would be cumbersome to display in full.

We will do this by using an alternative, but similarly defined YUI control: `ScrollingDataTable`.

Getting ready

Open `datatable.js` file for editing. We will modify the definition of the `dataTable` object.

How to do it...

Modify the `dataTable` definition to match the following code:

```
var dataTable = new YAHOO.widget.ScrollingDataTable
  ("container", columns, dataSource, {
    height: "150px"
});
```

How it works...

We used the alternative control `ScrollingDataTable`, passing in a configuration object as the fourth argument. This configuration object simply sets a height for the DataTable, and any content that overflows this height will scroll. Similarly, we may set a width to enable horizontal scrolling, or both a height and a width to enable both horizontal and vertical scrolling.

The following screenshots show that the content overflowing the set height of 150px is vertically scrollable:

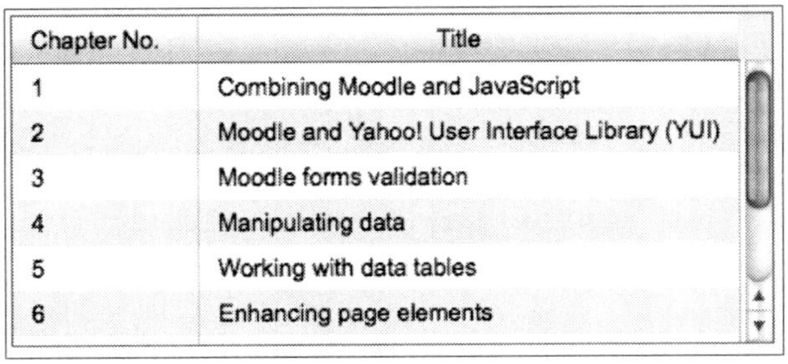

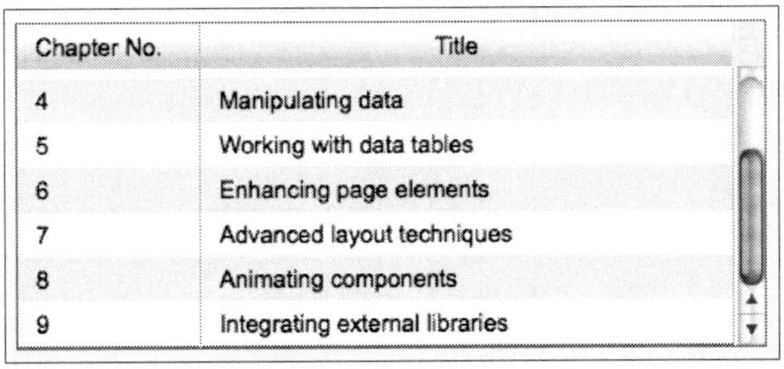

Chapter No.	Title
1	Combining Moodle and JavaScript
2	Moodle and Yahoo! User Interface Library (YUI)
3	Moodle forms validation
4	Manipulating data
5	Working with data tables
6	Enhancing page elements

Chapter No.	Title
4	Manipulating data
5	Working with data tables
6	Enhancing page elements
7	Advanced layout techniques
8	Animating components
9	Integrating external libraries

Enabling editing

The DataTable control has an inline-editing feature, which allows the user to click on any cell that has editing enabled and modify its value. This updates the underlying DataSource which can then be retrieved and stored.

Getting ready

Open the `datatable.js` file for editing. We will add some extra properties to the column definition, and also subscribe to the DataTable's `cellClickEvent`.

How to do it...

Modify the columns definition by adding the new `editor` property:

```
var columns = [
  {
     key: "chapter",
     label: "Chapter No.",
     formatter: "number",
     sortable: true,
     editor: new YAHOO.widget.TextboxCellEditor
        ({ validator: YAHOO.widget.DataTable.validateNumber } ),
  },
  {
     key: "title",
     label: "Title",
     formatter: "string",
     sortable: true,
     editor: new YAHOO.widget.TextboxCellEditor(),
  }
];
```

Next, we must enable editing by subscribing to the `cellClickEvent`. Add the following code after the definition of `dataTable`, as follows:

```
dataTable.subscribe("cellClickEvent", dataTable.
onEventShowCellEditor);
```

The following screenshot shows the cell editor in action:

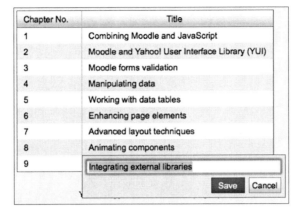

How it works...

We added the `editor` property to the column definitions of our table.

We used the `TextboxCellEditor` widget to provide the editing functionality. Additionally, we added a validator to the chapter number column to ensure that only valid numbers may be entered.

Finally, we subscribed to the DataTable's `cellClickEvent` event, to display the cell editor when the cell is clicked. The following screenshot shows the editor pops-up after we click on a particular cell:

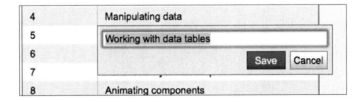

6
Enhancing Page Elements

In this chapter, we will cover:

- ▶ Adding a text box with auto-complete
- ▶ Adding a combo box with auto-complete
- ▶ Displaying auto-updating data
- ▶ Enabling resizable elements
- ▶ Adding custom tooltips
- ▶ Adding custom button controls

Introduction

The Yahoo! UI Library (YUI) offers a range of widgets and utilities to bring modern enhancements to your traditional page elements. In this chapter, we will look at a selection of these enhancements, including features often seen on modern interactive interfaces, such as:

- ▶ **Auto-complete**: This feature suggests possible values to the user by searching against a list of suggestions as they start typing. We will look at two different ways of using this. First, by providing suggestions as the user types into a text box, and second, by providing a list of possible values for them to select from a combo list box.

- ▶ **Auto-update**: This technique will allow us to update an area of the page based on a timed interval, which has many uses as we'll see. In this example, we will look at how to create a clock by updating the time on the page at one second intervals. This technique could also be used, for example, to update a news feed every minute, or update stock information every hour.

- ▸ **Resizable elements**: A simple enhancement which allows users to dynamically resize elements to suit their needs. This could be applied to elements containing a significant amount of text which would allow the user to control the width of the text to suit their personal preference for ideal readability.

- ▸ **Custom tooltips**: Tooltips appear when an element is hovered, displaying the associated title or alternative text (that is, a description of an image or the title of a hyperlink). This enhancement allows us to have more control over the look of the tooltips making them more visually appealing and more consistent with the overall look and feel of our page.

- ▸ **Custom buttons**: This enhancement allows us to completely restyle button elements, modifying their look and feel to be consistent with the rest of our page. This also allows us to have a consistent button style across different platforms and web browsers.

> We will once again be using mostly YUI Version 2 widgets and utilities within the YUI Version 3 framework. At the time of writing, few YUI2 widgets have been ported to YUI3. This method allows us the convenience of the improvements afforded by the YUI3 environment combined with the features of the widgets from YUI2.

Adding a text box with auto-complete

A common feature of many web forms is the ability to provide suggestions as the user types, based on a list of possible values. In this example, we enhance a standard HTML input text element with this feature.

This technique is useful in situations where we simply wish to offer suggestions to the user that they may or may not choose to select, that is, suggesting existing tags to be applied to a new blog post. They can either select a suggested value that matches one they have started typing, or simply continue typing a new, unused tag.

How to do it...

First, set up a basic Moodle page in the usual way. In this example, we create `autocomplete.php` with the following content:

```php
<?php
require_once(dirname(__FILE__) . '/../config.php');

$PAGE->set_context(get_context_instance(CONTEXT_SYSTEM));
$PAGE->set_url('/cook/autocomplete.php');
$PAGE->requires->js('/cook/autocomplete.js', true);

?>
```

```php
<?php
echo $OUTPUT->header();
?>
<div style="width:15em;height:10em;">
    <input id="txtInput" type="text">
    <div id="txtInput_container"></div>
</div>
<?php
echo $OUTPUT->footer();

?>
```

Secondly, we need to create our associated JavaScript file, autocomplete.js, with the following code:

```javascript
YUI().use("yui2-autocomplete", "yui2-datasource", function(Y) {

    var YAHOO = Y.YUI2;

    var dataSource = new YAHOO.util.LocalDataSource
    (
        ["Alpha","Bravo","Beta","Gamma","Golf"]
    );

    var autoCompleteText = new YAHOO.widget.AutoComplete("txtInput",
"txtInput_container", dataSource);

});
```

How it works...

Our HTML consists of three elements, a parent div element, and the other two elements contained within it: an input text box, and a placeholder div element to use to display the auto-complete suggestions.

Our JavaScript file then defines a DataSource to be used to provide suggestions, and then creates a new AutoComplete widget based on the HTML elements we have already defined.

In this example, we used a LocalDataSource for simplicity, but this may be substituted for any valid DataSource object, such as those we have covered in previous chapters.

Once we have a DataSource object available, we instantiate a new YUI2 AutoComplete widget, passing the following arguments:

- ▶ The name of the HTML input text element for which to provide auto-complete suggestions
- ▶ The name of the container element to use to display suggestions
- ▶ A valid data source object to use to find suggestions

Now when the user starts typing into the text box, any matching auto-complete suggestions are displayed and can be selected, as shown in the following screenshot:

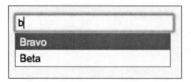

Adding a combo box with auto-complete

In this example, we will use auto-complete in conjunction with a combo box (drop-down list). This differs from the previous example in one significant way—it includes a drop-down arrow button that allows the user to see the complete list of values without typing first.

This is useful in situations where the user may be unsure of a suitable value. In this case, they can click the drop-down button to see suggestions without having to start guessing as they type. Additionally, this method also supports the same match-as-you-type style auto-complete as that of the previous recipe.

How to do it...

Open the `autocomplete.php` file from the previous recipe for editing, and add the following HTML below the text box based auto-complete control:

```
<div style="width:15em;height:10em;">
    <input id="txtCombo" type="text" style="vertical-align:top;position
:static;width:11em;"><span id="toggle"></span>
    <div id="txtCombo_container"></div>
</div>
```

Next, open the JavaScript file `autocomplete.js`, and modify it to match the following code:

```
YUI().use("yui2-autocomplete", "yui2-datasource", "yui2-element",
"yui2-button", "yui2-yahoo-dom-event", function(Y) {

 var YAHOO = Y.YUI2;

 var dataSource = new YAHOO.util.LocalDataSource
  (
     ["Alpha","Bravo","Beta","Gamma","Golf"]
  );

  var autoCompleteText = new YAHOO.widget.AutoComplete("txtInput",
    "txtInput_container", dataSource);

  var autoCompleteCombo = new YAHOO.widget.AutoComplete("txtCombo",
    "txtCombo_container", dataSource, {minQueryLength: 0,
```

```
      queryDelay: 0});
    var toggler = YAHOO.util.Dom.get("toggle");
    var tButton = new YAHOO.widget.Button({container:toggler,
      label:"&darr;"});

    var toggle = function(e) {
     if(autoCompleteCombo.isContainerOpen()) {
      autoCompleteCombo.collapseContainer();
     }
     else {
      autoCompleteCombo.getInputEl().focus();
      setTimeout(function() {
       autoCompleteCombo.sendQuery("");
      },0);
     }
    }
    tButton.on("click", toggle);
   });
```

You will notice that the HTML we added in this recipe is very similar to the last, with the exception that we included a `span` element just after the text box. This is used as a placeholder to insert a YUI2 button control.

This recipe is somewhat more complicated than the previous one, so we included some extra YUI2 modules: element, button, and yahoo-dom-event.

We define the AutoComplete widget in the same way as before, except we need to add two configuration options in an object passed as the fourth argument.

Next, we retrieve a reference to the button placeholder, and instantiate a new Button widget to use as the combo box 'drop-down' button.

Finally, we define a click handler for the button, and register it.

We now see the list of suggestions, which can be displayed by clicking on the drop-down button, as shown in the following screenshot:

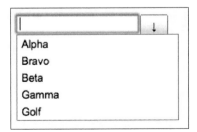

How it works...

The user can type into the box to receive auto-complete suggestions as before, but may now use the combo box style drop-down button instead to see a list of suggestions.

When the user clicks the drop-down button, the `click` event is fired.

This `click` event does the following:

▸ Hides the drop-down menu if it is displayed, which allows the user to toggle this list display on/off.

▸ If it is not displayed, it sets the focus to the text box (to allow the user to continue typing), and execute a blank query on the auto-complete widget, which will display the list of suggestions. Note that we explicitly enabled this blank query earlier when we defined the AutoComplete widget with the "minQueryLength: 0" option, which allowed queries of length 0 and above.

Displaying auto-updating data

Another useful interface enhancement is the ability to display data that is constantly updated at a set timed interval. For example, this could be used to update a list of news headlines every five minutes, or update the display of live stock data every minute.

In this recipe, we will take the basic example of a clock, displaying the full date and time on the page, and update it every second using the polling extension to the DataSource utility. This technique can be used to display any data from any data source, and update it as frequently as we like.

How to do it...

In this example, we will set up a very simple PHP page, `autoupdate.php`, containing only one placeholder `div` in which we will display the current date and time:

```php
<?php
require_once(dirname(__FILE__) . '/../config.php');
$PAGE->set_context(get_context_instance(CONTEXT_SYSTEM));
$PAGE->set_url('/cook/autoupdate.php');
$PAGE->requires->js('/cook/autoupdate.js', true);
echo $OUTPUT->header();
?>
<div id="txtUpdate"></div>
<?php
echo $OUTPUT->footer();
?>
```

Next, we define the associated JavaScript in `autoupdate.js`:

```
YUI().use("datasource-function", "datasource-polling", function(Y) {
  var getDateString = function()
  {
   return new Date();
  };
  var dataSource = new Y.DataSource.Function({source:getDateString});
  var   request =
  {
   callback :
   {
    success: function(e)
    {
     document.getElementById('txtUpdate').innerHTML =
       e.response.results[0];
    }
   }
  };
  var id = dataSource.setInterval(1000,request);
});
```

We have prepared a container element in the HTML in which to display the data.

We then define a DataSource object to use as the source of the data we will display. In this example, we used a `Function` data source, that is, a data source which simply uses the output of a native JavaScript function as its data (in this case, the current date and time). Once again, this data source can be substituted for any valid YUI data source, such as, a CSV of stock information or an RSS feed of news headlines.

Next, we define a request callback handler, which is used to display the data.

Finally, we register this handler with the DataSource object and configure it to poll (update) this data source every second (1,000 milliseconds).

How it works...

We have loaded two YUI modules: `datasource-function` and `datasource-polling`.

The first allows us to use a native JavaScript function as a DataSource, the second allows us to get the DataSource to update or 'poll' for new data as often as we specify.

The function data source we have defined simply returns the current date and time, and the callback handler simply writes the output into our container element.

All that is left is to use the `setInterval` method of the DataSource to register the defined callback function, and to configure it to update every 1,000 milliseconds (1 second).

We now see, upon loading the page, that the full current date and time is displayed, and updated every second, effectively creating a text based clock on the page, as shown in the following screenshot:

Sun Oct 03 2010 13:41:32 GMT+0100 (BST)

Enabling resizable elements

Another simple, but effective YUI2 utility is the `resize` utility. It has myriad uses from the simple (in this example, allowing a block of text to be resizable), to the more complicated scenarios (such as resizable form elements). It allows a user to change the size of the element in question by just dragging resize handles around the page, similar to how the user would resize any application window in an operating system's GUI. This is most useful when the element contains a large amount of content, allowing the user to size the element as required.

How to do it...

To begin, set up a simple page, `resize.php` with a block of text in a containing element, as follows:

```php
<?php
require_once(dirname(__FILE__) . '/../config.php');

$PAGE->set_context(get_context_instance(CONTEXT_SYSTEM));
$PAGE->set_url('/cook/resize.php');
$PAGE->requires->js('/cook/resize.js', true);

?>

<?php
echo $OUTPUT->header();
?>
<div id="content" style="width:20em;padding:1em;">
<p>
Moodle (abbreviation for Modular Object-Oriented Dynamic Learning
Environment) is a
free and open-source e-learning software platform, also known as a
Course Management System,
Learning Management System, or Virtual Learning Environment (VLE). As
of October 2010 it had
a user base of 49,952 registered and verified sites, serving 37
million users in 3.7 million
courses.</p>
```

```
</div>
<?php
echo $OUTPUT->footer();
?>
```

The associated JavaScript `resize.js` is very simple:

```
YUI().use("yui2-resize", function(Y) {
var YAHOO = Y.YUI2;
var resize = new YAHOO.util.Resize("content");
});
```

Instantiate a new `Resize` object, and pass the name of the element to make resizable as the only argument.

This allows the element to be resizable in both axes, with resize handles on the right and bottom of the element as seen in the following screenshot:

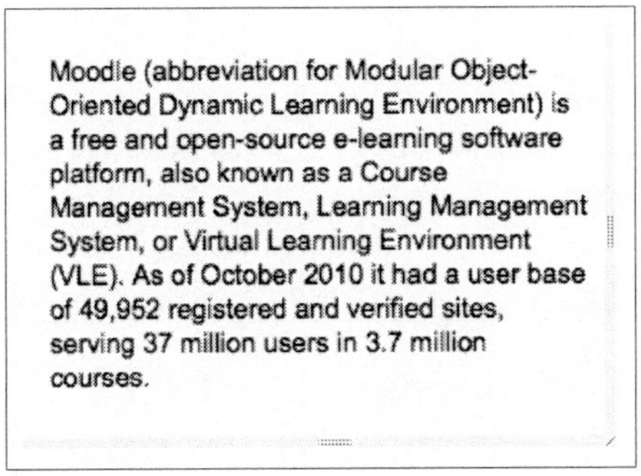

Moodle (abbreviation for Modular Object-Oriented Dynamic Learning Environment) is a free and open-source e-learning software platform, also known as a Course Management System, Learning Management System, or Virtual Learning Environment (VLE). As of October 2010 it had a user base of 49,952 registered and verified sites, serving 37 million users in 3.7 million courses.

How it works...

Instantiating the `Resize` control and passing the element to enhance in the constructor causes YUI to add resize handles to the element which allows it to be resized horizontally and vertically.

Adding custom tooltips

HTML tooltips, set up through the `title` attributes of elements, allow only text-based tooltips with no control over the layout. In this example, we will enhance an existing element with the YUI Tooltip widget.

How to do it...

To begin, set up a PHP page, `tooltip.php`, containing an image with the `title` attribute set:

```php
<?php
require_once(dirname(__FILE__) . '/../config.php');

$PAGE->set_context(get_context_instance(CONTEXT_SYSTEM));
$PAGE->set_url('/cook/tooltip.php');
$PAGE->requires->js('/cook/tooltip.js', true);

echo $OUTPUT->header();
?>
<img id="logo" src="../theme/image.php?theme=standard&image=moodlelo
go" title="Moodle Logo" />
<?php
echo $OUTPUT->footer();
?>
```

Next, set up the associated JavaScript file `tooltip.js`:

```javascript
YUI().use("yui2-yahoo-dom-event", "yui2-animation", "yui2-container",
function(Y) {

var YAHOO = Y.YUI2;

var toolTip = new YAHOO.widget.Tooltip("toolTip", {
    context: "logo"});

});
```

Create an element to which we will add a custom tooltip. In this example, we have only used an `img` tag with the title attribute set. Instantiate a new Tooltip widget, and pass the following two arguments:

1. The name of the tooltip object.
2. A configuration object, with the `context` property set to the name of the element to enhance.

How it works...

YUI "progressively enhances" the specified element by adding a custom tooltip element containing the original `title` text. Now when we hover over the image element to which we added the custom tooltip, we see the enhanced version appear, as shown in the following screenshot:

Moodle Logo

Adding custom button controls

YUI has a Button widget control, which offers many features for enhancing standard HTML button controls. It allows a great level of control over the look and function of the button, such as adding images, or allowing the button to have a label that differs from its value. In this example, we will enhance a basic HTML input button.

How to do it...

To begin, set up a PHP page, button.php, with an HTML input button control:

```php
<?php
require_once(dirname(__FILE__) . '/../config.php');

$PAGE->set_context(get_context_instance(CONTEXT_SYSTEM));
$PAGE->set_url('/cook/button.php');
$PAGE->requires->js('/cook/button.js', true);

?>
<?php
echo $OUTPUT->header();
?>
<input id="btnButton" type="button" value="Custom Button" />
<?php
echo $OUTPUT->footer();

?>
```

Next, define the associate JavaScript file button.js:

```javascript
YUI().use("yui2-button", function(Y) {

var YAHOO = Y.YUI2;

var customButton = new YAHOO.widget.Button("btnButton");

});
```

Instantiate a new Button widget control, and pass the ID of the button to enhance as the only argument. This then replaces the original element with a custom, skinned HTML button control that can now be customized further, as shown in the following screenshot:

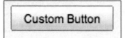

How it works...

The original HTML input button is replaced in the DOM by YUI with an HTML `button` control, wrapped in a placeholder `span` element. This can now be skinned or further enhanced with YUI button widget features.

7
Advanced Layout Techniques

In this chapter, we will cover:

- ▶ Adding a fly-out navigation menu
- ▶ Adding a drop-down navigation menu
- ▶ Displaying a tree-view navigation menu
- ▶ Adding a tabbed content control
- ▶ Displaying content in a modal window

Introduction

In this chapter, we will look at a selection of techniques available which are designed to enhance the way users interact with our content. First of all, we will look at the different ways we can present a navigation menu, giving the user a convenient list of the content that we are making available to them. Secondly, we will look at two different ways we can present the actual content to which they have navigated.

We will look at methods of enhancing the display and navigation of page content, by extending existing markup in keeping with the concept of 'progressive enhancement'. In this context, progressive enhancement essentially means that all the content will remain usable to users without JavaScript enabled, or without a suitably modern implementation of JavaScript enabled.

The concept of a navigation menu is well established in the realm of graphical user interfaces, and these tried and tested design patterns have been naturally carried over to the web. The three navigation design patterns that we will cover are as follows:

▶ Fly-out menu: A typical example of this design pattern is the context menu that is displayed when we right-click an object (for example, a file or folder).

▶ Drop-down menu: This design pattern will be familiar from its use within desktop applications, that is, the menu at the top of an application. This typically includes items such as File, Edit, Tools, and so on.

▶ Tree-view menu: This type of menu design pattern is often seen in file system browsers, as it is a natural way to display the hierarchy of files and folders that are contained within a file system.

There are many ways to organize the display of content beyond a linear collection of blocks. Again, well established techniques from traditional graphical user interfaces can be employed, such as the following:

▶ Tabbed content: This style of organizing content is most familiar from the tabbed features that are available in all of the most popular web browsers in use today.

▶ Modal windows: Most useful for displaying content that requires the immediate attention of the user. It appears above all other content and must be acknowledged by the user before they can resume interacting with the rest of the page.

Adding a fly-out navigation menu

The 'fly-out menu' style of navigation is one that many users will be familiar with. It has appeared in various guises in desktop operating system user interfaces and website user interfaces alike, allows a complex navigation tree to be displayed efficiently, and can be easily traversed by the user.

A typical example of this type of menu is the context-sensitive menu that is displayed when right-clicking almost any type of object in modern operating systems, including files, folders, blocks of highlighted text, and even directly on the desktop.

This example will build such a menu by extending existing HTML markup with the YUI3 module `node-menunav`.

How to do it...

1. We prepare a PHP page to house the markup of our menu. This example will use a file name `nav_flyout.php`, with the following content:

```php
<?php

require_once(dirname(__FILE__) . '/../config.php');
```

```php
$PAGE->set_context(get_context_instance(CONTEXT_SYSTEM));
$PAGE->set_url('/cook/nav_flyout.php');
$PAGE->requires->js('/cook/nav_flyout.js', true);

echo $OUTPUT->header();
?>
<div style="float:left;">
<div id="menu" class="yui3-menu">
 <div class="yui3-menu-content">
  <ul>

   <li class="yui3-menuitem">
    <a class="yui3-menuitem-content" href="#">Item 1</a>
   </li>
   <li class="yui3-menuitem">
    <a class="yui3-menuitem-content" href="#">Item 2</a>
   </li>

   <li>
    <a class="yui3-menu-label" href="#submenu-1">
     <em>Sub Menu</em>
    </a>
     <div id="submenu-1" class="yui3-menu">
      <div class="yui3-menu-content">
       <ul>
        <li class="yui3-menuitem">
         <a class="yui3-menuitem-content" href="#">Sub Item 1</a>
        </li>
        <li class="yui3-menuitem">
         <a class="yui3-menuitem-content" href="#">Sub Item 2</a>
        </li>
       </ul>
      </div>
     </div>
   </li>
   <li class="yui3-menuitem">
    <a class="yui3-menuitem-content"
       href="http://moodle.org/">Moodle.org</a>
   </li>
  </ul>
 </div>
</div>
</div>
<?php
```

```
echo $OUTPUT->footer();

?>
```

The HTML in this page primarily uses unordered lists to markup the navigation items, and different levels of the menu. The following screenshot shows the basic nested structure of the menu, prior to enhancement:

- Item 1
- Item 2
- *Sub Menu*

    - Sub Item 1
    - Sub Item 2

- Moodle.org

2. We will use an associated JavaScript file `nav_flyout.js` where we will enhance the menu markup into a functioning fly-out menu:

```
YUI().use("node-menunav", function(Y)
{
    Y.on("contentready", function ()
    {
        this.plug(Y.Plugin.NodeMenuNav);
    }, "#menu");
});
```

Now when we load the page, we see that the unordered lists in our markup are transformed into a dynamic fly-out navigation menu, as shown in the following screenshot:

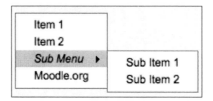

How it works...

In order for the JavaScript to correctly identify the components of our markup to use in the fly-out menu, we must set various IDs and CSS class names.

The first component is a main containing <div> element, to which we must assign an ID for use later in the JavaScript code. Additionally, the YUI3 module `node-menunav` dictates that we must assign this element a CSS class name of `yui3-menu`.

Directly inside the previous <div> element, we create a child <div> element that will be the container of the actual menu content. This requires the CSS class name `yui3-menu-content`.

The submenu now follows exactly the same format as the parent menu, where the ID of the containing <div> matches the target of the submenu label's `href` attribute.

The submenu structure may be repeated recursively as necessary, to reflect the required number of levels of navigation.

Once we have defined the markup of our hierarchical menu, the hard work is over, and YUI3 does the rest.

The JavaScript in this example firstly uses the `on-contentready` event of our menu to ensure that the markup is fully loaded and rendered within the DOM before attempting to extend it.

Finally, the `NodeMenuNav` plug-in is applied to our menu, and the fly-out menu is automatically built for us based on all the IDs and CSS classes we defined in the markup.

Adding a drop-down navigation menu

A slight variation to the fly-out menu is the drop-down menu. Again, this is a menu structure that many users will find familiar and will be able to use comfortably.

Getting ready

We may build on the previous recipe, as the markup will be almost identical, just with the addition of some CSS class names applied to the parent element.

How to do it...

1. This example uses a file `nav_dropdown.php` with the following content:

```php
<?php

require_once(dirname(__FILE__) . '/../config.php');

$PAGE->set_context(get_context_instance(CONTEXT_SYSTEM));
$PAGE->set_url('/cook/nav_dropdown.php');
$PAGE->requires->js('/cook/nav_dropdown.js', true);

echo $OUTPUT->header();

?>

<div id="menu" class="yui3-menu yui3-menu-horizontal yui3-
    menubuttonnav" style="float:left;height:100px;">
  <div class="yui3-menu-content">
```

```html
<ul>
  <li class="yui3-menuitem">
   <a class="yui3-menuitem-content" href="#">Item 1</a>
  </li>
  <li class="yui3-menuitem">
   <a class="yui3-menuitem-content" href="#">Item 2</a>
  </li>

  <li>
   <a class="yui3-menu-label" href="#submenu-1">
    <em>Sub Menu</em>
   </a>
   <div id="submenu-1" class="yui3-menu">
    <div class="yui3-menu-content">
     <ul>
       <li class="yui3-menuitem">
        <a class="yui3-menuitem-content" href="#">Sub Item 1</a>
       </li>
       <li class="yui3-menuitem">
        <a class="yui3-menuitem-content" href="#">Sub Item 2</a>
       </li>

     </ul>
    </div>
   </div>
  </li>
  <li class="yui3-menuitem">
   <a class="yui3-menuitem-content"
      href="http://moodle.org/">Moodle.org
   </a>
  </li>
 </ul>
 </div>
</div>
<?php
echo $OUTPUT->footer();

?>
```

This markup produces a simple list-based layout structure for the navigation menu, as shown in the following screenshot prior to any styling or JavaScript enhancement:

- Item 1
- Item 2
- *Sub Menu*

    - Sub Item 1
    - Sub Item 2

- Moodle.org

2. We require the associated JavaScript `nav_dropdown.js` with the following content:

```
YUI().use("node-menunav", function(Y)
{
    Y.on("contentready", function ()
    {
        this.plug(Y.Plugin.NodeMenuNav);
    }, "#menu");
});
```

 Note: the JavaScript used in this example is identical to that used in the fly-out menu example.

The menu is transformed into a drop-down menu simply by the addition of the following CSS classes to the parent menu <div> element:

Name	Purpose
`yui3-menu-horizontal`	Instructs YUI3 to build a horizontal 'drop-down' menu rather than the default 'fly-out' menu.
`yui3-menubuttonnav`	Causes the menu items to behave like buttons, providing a more familiar 'feel' to the menu by adding visual cues such as borders and arrow icons.

How it works...

The transformation from vertical fly-out menu to horizontal drop-down menu is configured purely through the addition of CSS classes as described earlier in this chapter, and YUI3 takes care of everything for us. The following screenshot shows the final rendering of the drop-down menu:

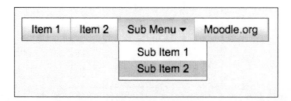

Displaying a tree-view navigation menu

Yet another method of displaying a navigational hierarchy is the tree-view. This is familiar to users from cases such as browsing a directory structure of files and folders within a graphical operating system shell (for example, Microsoft Windows Explorer).

At the time of writing, YUI3 lacks a stable port of the TreeView widget so we will be using the TreeView widget from YUI2.

How to do it...

1. We must define the markup of our menu tree, in this example within `nav_tree.php`:

```php
<?php
require_once(dirname(__FILE__) . '/../config.php');

$PAGE->set_context(get_context_instance(CONTEXT_SYSTEM));
$PAGE->set_url('/cook/nav_tree.php');
$PAGE->requires->js('/cook/nav_tree.js', true);

echo $OUTPUT->header();
?>
  <div id="treeContainer">
   <ul>
     <li><a href="#">Item 1</a></li>
     <li><a href="#">Item 2</a></li>
     <li>Sub Tree
      <ul>
        <li><a href="#">Sub Item 1</a></li>
        <li><a href="#">Sub Item 2</a></li>
      </ul>
```

```
    </li>
    <li><a href="http://moodle.org/">Moodle.org</a></li>
  </ul>
 </div>
<?php

echo $OUTPUT->footer();

?>
```

The following screenshot shows the basic hierarchical structure of the markup using standard unordered lists, prior to enhancement:

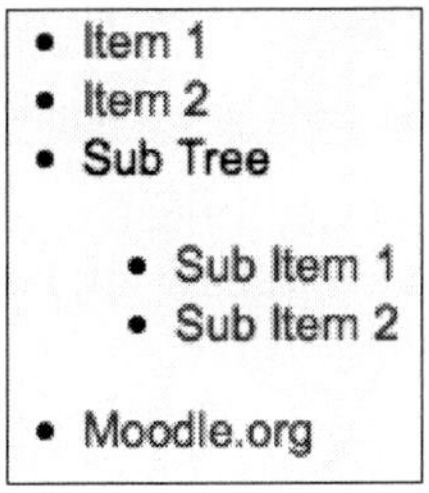

2. Next, we add the necessary code to our associated JavaScript file, `nav_tree.js`, with the following content:

```
YUI().use("yui2-treeview", function(Y)
{
    var YAHOO = Y.YUI2;

    var treeView = new YAHOO.widget.TreeView("treeContainer");
    treeView.render();

});
```

How it works...

First, we create a container <div> to house the menu, setting an ID to use as a reference in our JavaScript. Inside this container, we build a standard hierarchy of unordered lists as required.

Next, we initialize the YUI2 module 'treeview' within our YUI3 code, and instantiate a new TreeView widget, passing the ID of the containing <div> in our markup.

Finally, we call the render method of this new TreeView widget object.

The YUI2 TreeView module automatically renders our unordered list in the container element we specified in the constructor when we call the render element.

Our unordered list is then hidden and replaced with a dynamic tree-view representation of the original list, as shown in the following screenshot:

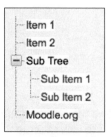

Adding a tabbed content control

A tabbed content control is a convenient way for users to navigate a series of panels of content within a single page. This recipe will show you how to use the YUI3 TabView module to enhance a series of <div> content panels.

How to do it...

1. First, we define the markup that we will enhance, in this example, `tabview.php`:

```php
<?php
    require_once(dirname(__FILE__) . '/../config.php');

    $PAGE->set_context(get_context_instance(CONTEXT_SYSTEM));
    $PAGE->set_url('/cook/tabview.php');
    $PAGE->requires->js('/cook/tabview.js', true);

    echo $OUTPUT->header();
?>
<div id="tabContainer" style="width:400px">
 <ul>
  <li><a href="#tab1">Moodle</a></li>
  <li><a href="#tab2">Origins</a></li>
  <li><a href="#tab3">Origin of the name</a></li>
 </ul>
 <div>
  <div id="tab1">
          Moodle (abbreviation for Modular Object-Oriented
          Dynamic Learning Environment) is a free and open-source
e-learning
          software platform, also known as a Course Management
System, Learning
          Management System, or Virtual Learning Environment
(VLE). As of
```

```
                October 2010 it had a user base of 49,952 registered
and verified
                sites, serving 37 million users in 3.7 million courses.
   </div>
   <div id="tab2">
                Martin Dougiamas, who has graduate degrees in computer
science and
                education, wrote the first version of Moodle. Dougiamas
started a
                Ph.D. to examine "The use of Open Source software to
support a
                social constructionist epistemology of teaching and
learning
                within Internet-based communities of reflective
inquiry". Although
                how exactly social constructionism makes Moodle
different from other
                eLearning platforms is difficult to show, it has been
cited as an
                important factor by Moodle adopters. Other Moodle
adopters,
                such as the Open University in the UK, have pointed out
that Learning
                Management Systems can equally be seen as "relatively
pedagogy-neutral"
   </div>
   <div id="tab3">
                The acronym Moodle stands for Modular Object-Oriented
Dynamic Learning
                Environment (in the early years the "M" stood for
"Martin's", named after
                Martin Dougiamas, the original developer). As well as
being an acronym,
                the name was chosen because of the dictionary
definition of Moodle
                and to correspond to an available domain name.
   </div>
  </div>
</div>

<?php
   echo $OUTPUT->footer();
?>
```

Prior to enhancement, this produces a linear series of content blocks, as shown in the following screenshot:

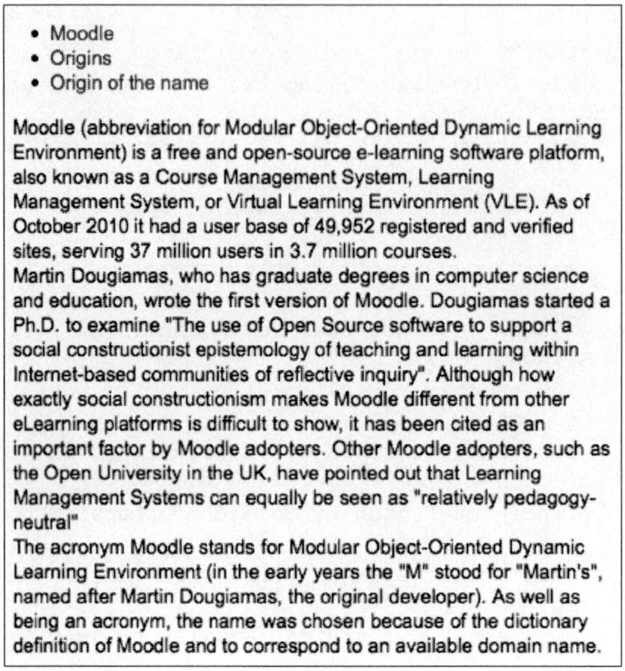

- Moodle
- Origins
- Origin of the name

Moodle (abbreviation for Modular Object-Oriented Dynamic Learning Environment) is a free and open-source e-learning software platform, also known as a Course Management System, Learning Management System, or Virtual Learning Environment (VLE). As of October 2010 it had a user base of 49,952 registered and verified sites, serving 37 million users in 3.7 million courses.

Martin Dougiamas, who has graduate degrees in computer science and education, wrote the first version of Moodle. Dougiamas started a Ph.D. to examine "The use of Open Source software to support a social constructionist epistemology of teaching and learning within Internet-based communities of reflective inquiry". Although how exactly social constructionism makes Moodle different from other eLearning platforms is difficult to show, it has been cited as an important factor by Moodle adopters. Other Moodle adopters, such as the Open University in the UK, have pointed out that Learning Management Systems can equally be seen as "relatively pedagogy-neutral"

The acronym Moodle stands for Modular Object-Oriented Dynamic Learning Environment (in the early years the "M" stood for "Martin's", named after Martin Dougiamas, the original developer). As well as being an acronym, the name was chosen because of the dictionary definition of Moodle and to correspond to an available domain name.

2. We then add the necessary code to the associated JavaScript file `tabview.js`:

```
YUI().use("tabview", function(Y)
{
    var tabView = new Y.TabView
    (
        {
            srcNode: '#tabContainer'
        }
    );

    tabView.render();

});
```

How it works...

The markup consists of a parent <div> container, to which we must assign an ID for use later as a reference in the JavaScript code.

This <div> then contains firstly an unordered list, with an item for each tab. Each item is an <a> tag with the text being the label for the tab, and the `href` referring to the ID of a <div> content panel defined later.

Next comes another <div> container, which will contain one child <div> for each tab of content. The ID of each of these child <div> containers will match that of the `href` of the corresponding item in the unordered list defined earlier.

Moving on to the JavaScript code, we load the YUI3 module 'TabView' first. Next, we create a new instance of the TabView module, passing a configuration object to the constructor. This configuration object contains a single property in this example—(`srcNode`) this is simply set to the ID of the parent <div> of our tabbed content markup.

Finally, we call the `render` method of this new TabView object, and our markup is transformed from one block of text into individual tabs that can be clicked through one at a time, as shown in the following screenshot:

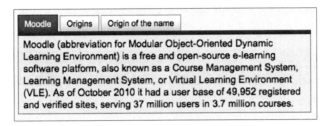

The following screenshot shows the content when the **Origins** tab is clicked:

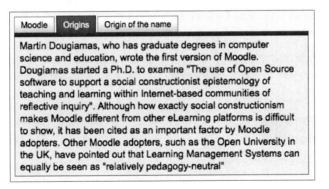

The following screenshot shows the content when the **Origin of the name** tab is clicked:

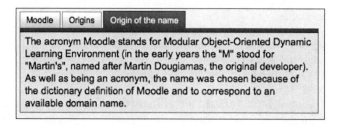

When we create a new TabView object, we instruct which element to use as the base by specifying the ID in the `srcNode` property of the configuration object.

The TabView module then identifies the unordered list inside this containing element and uses it to generate the navigation tabs for the content.

When the tabs are clicked, the module displays the corresponding content <div> element by matching the `href` of the tab to the ID of the content element.

Displaying content in a modal window

The modal window is another user interface element which has seen widespread use in both operating system and website interfaces alike.

If a window is described as 'modal' this means it will temporarily block the user from accessing other parts of the application until the window has been closed. This is useful when the application requires some input from the user (for example, Yes/No confirmation) before the current workflow may continue.

This example will show how to display content in a Modal window, overlaying all current page content. We will make use of the container module from YUI2 in lieu of any alternative native to YUI3 at the time of writing.

How to do it...

1. First, we define the necessary markup, in this example, `modal.php`:

```php
<?php
    require_once(dirname(__FILE__) . '/../config.php');

    $PAGE->set_context(get_context_instance(CONTEXT_SYSTEM));
    $PAGE->set_url('/cook/modal.php');
    $PAGE->requires->js('/cook/modal.js', true);

    echo $OUTPUT->header();
?>
```

```
<input type="button" id="show" value="Show panel" />
<div id="modalContainer">
<div id="modalPanel">
 <div class="hd">Moodle</div>
   <div class="bd">
       Moodle (abbreviation for Modular Object-Oriented
       Dynamic Learning Environment) is a free and open-source
e-learning
       software platform, also known as a Course Management System,
Learning
       Management System, or Virtual Learning Environment (VLE). As
of
       October 2010 it had a user base of 49,952 registered and
verified
       sites, serving 37 million users in 3.7 million courses.
   </div>
   <div class="ft">[Footer]</div>
</div>
</div>
<?php
   echo $OUTPUT->footer();
?>
```

Before we convert this HTML markup into a fully functional modal window, it renders as nothing more than a button and a block of un-styled text, as shown in the following screenshot:

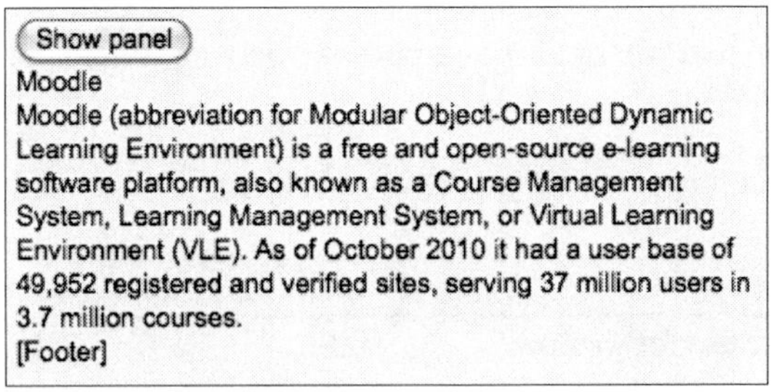

2. Next, we define the JavaScript necessary for rendering this markup in the form of a modal window, in `modal.js`:

```
YUI().use("yui2-container", "yui2-dragdrop", "node", function(Y)
{
    var YAHOO = Y.YUI2;

    var panel = new YAHOO.widget.Panel("modalPanel",
        {
```

```
                visible:false,
                modal:true,
                width:"300px",
                height:"auto",
                 close: true,
                 draggable: false,
                 fixedcenter: true
         }
    );

    panel.hideEvent.subscribe(function()
    {
        Y.one('#modalContainer').setStyle('height', null);
    });

    panel.render();

    function showPanel()
    {
        Y.one('#modalContainer').setStyle('height',Y.one('body').get
            ('winHeight'));
        panel.show();
    }

    Y.on('click', showPanel, "#show");

});
```

How it works...

Our content is defined in markup by way of a parent <div> container to which we assign an ID as a reference.

This parent container contains three child <div> elements:

Purpose	CSS Class name required
Header text for window	hd
Main window body content	bd
Footer text for window	ft

We must now instantiate a new Panel widget in our JavaScript, passing a configuration object with the following properties:

Name	Value	Description
visible	false	Hides the window by default
modal	true	Sets the window behavior to modal
width	300px	Sets desired width of window
height	150px	Sets desired height of window
close	true	Displays a close button in the top-right corner of the window
draggable	true	Allows the window to be moved by dragging
fixedcenter	true	Displays the window in the center of the viewport

Next, we will subscribe to the panel's hide event. The function we define here will be called whenever the window has been hidden, that is, when the user has clicked the window's close icon. In this function, we will reset the height of the <div> element that contains the modal panel, restoring it to its original height.

Next, we call the render method of the new instance of the Panel widget.

Finally, we define a function to display the window. In this example, we will attach that to the click, even of our **Show panel** button.

When the page is loaded, our JavaScript hides our window content, and renders it into a modal type window.

When the user clicks the **Show panel** button, the window's show method is called. First, the containing <div> element's height is set to match the height of the browser window and to ensure that the modal panel is not clipped and is displayed in its entirety, as shown in the following screenshot:

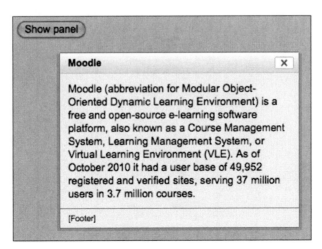

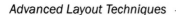

Note the background content is grayed-out and is inaccessible to the user until the window is dismissed, in accordance with the modal concept. This allows the designer to ensure that the user considers any particularly important information or required actions immediately, before they resume their interaction with the rest of the page.

8
Animating Components

In this chapter, we will cover:

- ▶ Fading in an element
- ▶ Fading out an element
- ▶ Scrolling an element
- ▶ Resizing an element
- ▶ Animating with Easing
- ▶ Moving an element along a straight path
- ▶ Moving an element along a curved path
- ▶ Changing an element's color
- ▶ Sequencing multiple animations

Introduction

In this chapter, we will look at how to bring elements on our pages to life with the use of animation. You must take a rational approach when it comes to where and when to add animation into your pages. Try to keep the use of animation only to situations where it will benefit the users' experience, and avoid bombarding them with animations that serve no purpose.

Animation can provide beneficial effects in a range of situations such as easing the transition from one element to another by fading opacity, or by changing the color of an element that requires the user's attention by gently pulsing from a light to a dark shade.

We will be using the animation capabilities built into the YUI3 library, which is included in the standard Moodle installation. The basis for all animation consists of changing the value of an element's attributes from one specific value to another, over a specified time span. For example, to fade-out an element we may change the element's opacity from 100% to 0%, or to move an element's position we may change its X and Y coordinates.

 Carefully consider when and where to use animation. Ask yourself, "Will this improve the user experience?" Avoid unnecessary animations, as they will simply distract the user and degrade the usability of your page.

Fading in an element

In this recipe, we will produce a fade-in effect by animating a change in opacity of the element from 0% to 100%. This offers a more subtle approach to making an element visible than simply changing from invisible to visible, or from not displayed to displayed.

Here we can see the key steps in this animation by looking at a selection of frames:

Animation: Fade-in

Animation: Fade-in

How to do it...

We begin by creating a PHP page to load the Moodle programming environment, which in turn loads the YUI3 environment with which we will be working.

In the following example, we create an anim_fadein.php file with the following content:

```php
<?php
require_once(dirname(__FILE__) . '/../config.php');
$PAGE->set_context(get_context_instance(CONTEXT_SYSTEM));
$PAGE->set_url('/cook/anim_fadein.php');
$PAGE->requires->js('/cook/anim_fadein.js', true);
echo $OUTPUT->header();
?>
<div id="anim-container" style="border:1px solid black;background-colo
r:#0099FF;float:left;padding:30px;opacity:0;">
<h1>Animation: Fade-in</h1>
</div>
<?php
echo $OUTPUT->footer();
?>
```

Additionally, we create a JavaScript file where we will perform the animation. In this example, anim_fadein.js, with the following content:

```javascript
YUI().use("node", "anim", function(Y) {
    var anim = new Y.Anim({
            node: '#anim-container',
            to: {
             opacity:1
            }
    });
    Y.on("contentready", function ()
```

```
    {
        anim.run();
    }, "#anim-container");

});
```

How it works...

As a starting point, we require an element in our page that we wish to "fade-in". Additionally, we ensure that the element starts hidden by setting the CSS attribute 'opacity' to 0.

Next, we need to add the necessary JavaScript code to change the opacity from 0 to 1. We begin by creating a new YUI3 instance, and by loading two modules: `node` and `anim`.

The `node` module allows us access to attach events to our page, and the `anim` module provides us access to YUI3's animation capability.

We have now loaded the necessary modules and we can create a new instance of the `anim` module, passing in several parameters. The `node` parameter is the ID of the element we wish to animate, and the `to` parameter is an object containing the attributes we wish to animate, that is, the final values of the attributes we are changing over time.

In this example, we just include the opacity attribute in the `to` parameter, and set it to `1`, that is, to 100%.

Finally, we subscribe to the `contentready` event of the element we are animating. This ensures that the element will be loaded completely and is available for use before the attached code runs. The code we attach here simply calls the `run` method of the `anim` object we created earlier in the code.

When the element we have chosen to animate has finished loading in the page, the `contentready` event is fired, which is where we made a call to the animation object's `run` method. The `run` method now performs the transformation we specified earlier, that is, to change the opacity to 1. We have not specified the duration for the transformation, so it defaults to 1 second. This means the element's opacity will change from 0% to 100% over a 1 second time span.

Fading out an element

In this recipe, we will produce a fade-out effect by animating a change in opacity of the element from 100% to 0%. This offers a more subtle approach to making an element become invisible than simply using CSS to change the visibility or display properties to hidden or none.

We can see the key steps in this animation by looking at the following selection of frames:

How to do it...

We begin by creating a PHP page to load the Moodle programming environment, which in turn loads the YUI3 environment with which we will be working.

In this example, we create an anim_fadeout.php file with the following content:

```php
<?php
require_once(dirname(__FILE__) . '/../config.php');
$PAGE->set_context(get_context_instance(CONTEXT_SYSTEM));
$PAGE->set_url('/cook/anim_fadeout.php');
$PAGE->requires->js('/cook/anim_fadeout.js', true);
echo $OUTPUT->header();
?>
<div id="anim-container" style="border:1px solid black;background-colo
r:#0099FF;float:left;padding:30px;">
<h1>Animation: Fade-out</h1>
```

```
</div>
<?php
echo $OUTPUT->footer();

?>
```

Additionally, we create a JavaScript file where we will perform the animation. In this example, anim_fadeout.js with the following content:

```
YUI().use("node", "anim", function(Y) {

    var anim = new Y.Anim({
            node: '#anim-container',
            to: {
             opacity:0
             }
    });

    Y.on("contentready", function ()
    {
        anim.run();
    }, "#anim-container");

});
```

How it works...

As a starting point, we require an element in our page that we wish to "fade-out". Obviously, all elements default to 100% opacity, so we need not specify this explicitly.

Next, we need to add the necessary JavaScript code to change the opacity from 1 to 0. We begin by creating a new YUI3 instance and loading two modules: node and anim.

The node module allows us access to attach events to our page and the anim module provides us access to YUI3's animation capability.

Now that we have loaded the necessary modules, we can create a new instance of the anim module, passing in several parameters. The node parameter is the ID of the element we wish to animate, and the to parameter is an object containing the attributes we wish to animate, that is, the final values of the attributes we are changing over time.

In this example, we simply include the opacity attribute in the to parameter, and set it to 0, that is, to 0%.

Finally, we subscribe to the contentready event of the element we are animating. This ensures that the element will be loaded completely and is available for use before the attached code runs. The code we attach here simply calls the run method of the anim object we created earlier in the code.

When the element we have chosen to animate has finished loading the page, the `contentready` event is fired, which is where we made a call to the animation object's `run` method. The `run` method now performs the transformation we specified earlier, that is, to change the opacity to 0. We have not specified the duration for the transformation, so it defaults to 1 second; meaning the element's opacity will change from 100% to 0% over a 1 second time span.

Scrolling an element

In this recipe, we will look at how to animate the scrolling of content within a container element. We will scroll the content of a `div` tag, that is, the width and height that have been set to force the content to overflow, and also set that overflow to be hidden.

We can see the key steps in this animation by looking at the following selection of frames:

How to do it...

We begin by creating a PHP page to set up a basic Moodle programming environment, in this case, `anim_scroll.php`, with the following content:

```php
<?php

require_once(dirname(__FILE__) . '/../config.php');

$PAGE->set_context(get_context_instance(CONTEXT_SYSTEM));
$PAGE->set_url('/cook/anim_scroll.php');
$PAGE->requires->js('/cook/anim_scroll.js', true);

echo $OUTPUT->header();
?>
<div id="anim-container" style="border:1px solid black;background-col
or:#0099FF;float:left;padding:5px;width:120px;height:200px;overflow:h
idden;">

<h1>Animation: Scroll</h1>
<p>
    Moodle (abbreviation for Modular Object-Oriented
    Dynamic Learning Environment) is a free and open-source
    e-learning software platform, also known as a Course
    Management System, Learning Management System, or
    Virtual Learning Environment (VLE). As of October
    2010 it had a user base of 49,952 registered and
    verified sites, serving 37 million users in 3.7 million
    courses.
</p>
<p>
    Moodle was originally developed by Martin Dougiamas
    to help educators create online courses with a focus on
    interaction and collaborative construction of content,
    and is in continual evolution.
</p>
</div>
<?php

echo $OUTPUT->footer();

?>
```

We also create an associated JavaScript file, `anim_scroll.js`, where we will add the animation code, with the following content:

```javascript
YUI().use("node", "anim", function(Y) {

    var anim = new Y.Anim({
            node: '#anim-container',
```

```
          duration:'3'
    });
    Y.on("contentready", function ()
    {
        var yScrollHeight =
          Y.one('#anim-container').get('scrollHeight');

        var yClientHeight =
          Y.one('#anim-container').get('clientHeight');

        var yScroll = yScrollHeight-yClientHeight;

        anim.set('to', { scroll: [0, yScroll] });

        anim.run();
    }, "#anim-container");

});
```

How it works...

The basis for this scroll animation is to have an element that has contents that overflow its bounds. In other words, we have a `div` tag that contains paragraphs of text which will not fit inside the width and height that has been set. In this case, we have set the CSS attribute `overflow` to hidden. This tells the browser to simply hide the content that will not fit. Alternatively, we could set this value to `scroll` if we wished for users to be able to scroll the content manually in addition to the scroll being animated.

Moving on to the JavaScript code, we first load the required YUI3 modules, namely `node` and `anim`. Next, we instantiate (create) a new `anim` object, passing the ID of our `div` tag. We are also setting the duration here to be longer than the default of one second, allowing the content to scroll more smoothly over three seconds.

Next, we again subscribe to the `contentready` event of our element, to ensure that it is loaded completely before we try and animate it. We start by retrieving both the `scrollHeight` and the `clientHeight` values of the container. The `scrollHeight` gives the full height of all the content inside the container, and the `clientHeight` gives the height of the content that is currently visible on screen. To find the value we need to scroll to, in order to reach the end of the content, we simply subtract the visible height from the full height, that is, (scrollHeight – clientHeight).

Next, we add a call to the `set` method of the `anim` object. Here, we add a `to` property, specifying the X and Y coordinates of our final scroll position. This is done by passing an object with a `scroll` property with its value set to an array with two values, first the X coordinate, and second the Y coordinate for the final scroll position. We have set the Y coordinate to 0, as we are not performing any horizontal scroll, this will not change. Finally, we set the X coordinate to be equal to the scroll distance we calculated earlier.

When the container `div` is fully loaded, through the `contentready` event, we take the necessary height measurements in order to calculate the Y coordinate of the end of the content that we wish to scroll to, and add this to the animation object through the `set` method. Finally, we call the `run` method which activates the animation, scrolling the content all the way to the end over the duration of three seconds as we specified.

Resizing an element

In this recipe, we will cover how to resize an element on screen by animating a change in its height and width. We will resize a container `div`, enlarging both the width and height.

Here we can see the key steps in this animation by looking at a selection of frames:

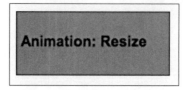

How to do it...

We begin by creating a PHP page to set up a basic Moodle programming environment. In this case, `anim_resize.php`, with the following content:

```php
<?php
require_once(dirname(__FILE__) . '/../config.php');
$PAGE->set_context(get_context_instance(CONTEXT_SYSTEM));
$PAGE->set_url('/cook/anim_resize.php');
$PAGE->requires->js('/cook/anim_resize.js', true);
echo $OUTPUT->header();
```

```
?>
<div id="anim-container" style="border:1px solid black;background-colo
r:#0099FF;float:left;padding:5px;">

<h1>Animation: Resize</h1>

</div>
<?php
echo $OUTPUT->footer();

?>
```

We also create an associated JavaScript file, `anim_resize.js`, where we will add the animation code, with the following content:

```
YUI().use("node", "anim", function(Y) {

var anim = new Y.Anim({
        node: '#anim-container',
        to: {
         width:'300px',
         height:'100px'
         }
});
    Y.on("contentready", function ()
    {
       anim.run();
    }, "#anim-container");

});
```

How it works...

We begin with a container element, in this case, a `div` element, that has been set to shrink its width to fit the content by setting the CSS attribute float to the left. Similarly, the height will also shrink to fit the contents.

We then set up an `anim` object to transform the height and width to new larger values, thus enlarging the container `div`.

The `div` element starts with its default "shrink to fit" dimensions. We create an `anim` object that will enlarge the width and height to 300px and 100px respectively.

We set the animation to run when the content has loaded with the `contentready` event. This causes the element to animate its expansion to its new dimensions over the default time span of 1 second.

Animating with easing

Animation easing is the technique of adding acceleration or deceleration at different points during the animation to provide smoother transitions. It may also cause the transformation to exceed the destined value before returning to its final state. For example, when animating a change in height of an element, a *bouncing* effect could be achieved by causing the animation to overshoot the final value, then undershoot, then settle at the final value.

Fortunately, YUI3 includes many built-in easing types that we can add to our animations with very little extra code. In this example, we will use the *bounce-out* easing behavior in conjunction with a resize animation. This will make the bounds of the box appear to bounce as they reach the end of the animation.

A complete list of the many easing behaviors that are available in YUI3 is available at the following URL:

`http://developer.yahoo.com/yui/3/api/Easing.html`

Here, we can see the key steps in this animation by looking at a selection of frames:

Animation: Resize with easing

Animation: Resize with easing

Animation: Resize with easing

Animation: Resize with easing

How to do it...

We begin by creating a PHP page to set up a basic Moodle programming environment. In this case, `anim_ease.php`, with the following content:

```php
<?php
require_once(dirname(__FILE__) . '/../config.php');

$PAGE->set_context(get_context_instance(CONTEXT_SYSTEM));
$PAGE->set_url('/cook/anim_ease.php');
$PAGE->requires->js('/cook/anim_ease.js', true);

echo $OUTPUT->header();

?>
<div id="anim-container" style="border:1px solid black;background-colo
r:#0099FF;float:left;padding:5px;">

<h1>Animation: Resize with easing</h1>

</div>
<?php

echo $OUTPUT->footer();

?>
```

We also create an associated JavaScript file, `anim_ease.js`, where we will add the animation code, with the following content:

```javascript
YUI().use("node", "anim", function(Y) {

var anim = new Y.Anim({
        node: '#anim-container',
        to: {
         width:'400px',
         height:'100px'
         },
        easing:Y.Easing.bounceOut
});

   Y.on("contentready", function ()
   {
     anim.run();
   }, "#anim-container");

});
```

How it works...

We created a resize animation in the same way as in the previous recipe, enlarging the width and height of a container `div`.

In this recipe, we added an extra property `easing` to the `anim` object to perform the easing. This takes a value in the form of any of the YUI easing behaviors which are available under the `Y.Easing` object, in this case, `Y.Easing.bounceOut`.

Now when our resize animation is run from the container `div`'s `contentready` event, it performs the animation with a bouncing effect at the end of the animation in accordance with the behavior of the `bounceOut` easing.

Moving an element along a straight path

An element can be repositioned by moving it along a straight path by animating a change in its X and Y position on the page. In this recipe, we will animate the moving of a container `div` element 200 pixels to the right.

Here, we can see the key steps in this animation by looking at a selection of frames:

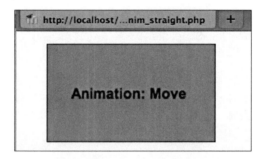

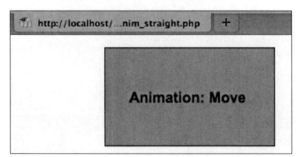

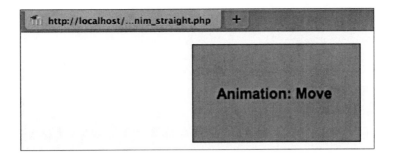

How to do it...

We begin by creating a PHP page to set up a basic Moodle programming environment. In this case, anim_straight.php, with the following content:

```php
<?php
require_once(dirname(__FILE__) . '/../config.php');

$PAGE->set_context(get_context_instance(CONTEXT_SYSTEM));
$PAGE->set_url('/cook/anim_straight.php');
$PAGE->requires->js('/cook/anim_straight.js', true);

echo $OUTPUT->header();
?>
<div id="anim-container" style="border:1px solid black;background-colo
r:#0099FF;padding:30px;width:150px;">

<h1>Animation: Move</h1>

</div>
<?php
echo $OUTPUT->footer();

?>
```

We also create an associated JavaScript file anim_straight.js, where we will add the animation code, with the following content:

```javascript
YUI().use("anim", function(Y) {

var anim = new Y.Anim({
        node: '#anim-container'
});

    Y.on("contentready", function ()
    {
        var startX = Y.one('#anim-container').getX();
        var startY = Y.one('#anim-container').getY();
        anim.set('to', { xy:[startX+200, startY] });
```

```
        anim.run();
    }, "#anim-container");
});
```

How it works...

We start with a `div` container element in the HTML that we will move to a new position.

Moving on to the JavaScript code, we begin by creating a new `anim` object, passing the ID of our `div` element to the node property.

Next, we subscribe to the `div`'s `contentready` event and add code that will run only when the div has been completely loaded in the browser.

First, we get the current X and Y coordinates of the `div` so we know where the motion will begin. Next, we call the `set` method of our `anim` object which allows us to set the `to` property to new X and Y coordinates. We will move the `div` to the right by 200px, so we add that distance to its current X coordinate, and leave the Y coordinate unchanged, as we will not be moving the `div` up or down.

When the `div` is loaded completely, our code retrieves the current X and Y coordinates, and modifies them to the new values. In this case, adding 200px to the X coordinate, and leaving the Y coordinate unchanged. This has the effect of animating the `div` moving 200px to the right, over the default time span of 1 second.

Moving an element along a curved path

Another way to animate motion of an element from one position to another is to use a curve motion animation. The curve is specified as a matrix of X and Y coordinates which the element's motion will follow.

In this recipe, we will move a `div` across a simple curve, with two sets of X and Y coordinates in the matrix list.

Here, we can see the key steps in this animation by looking at a selection of frames:

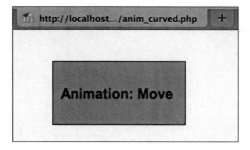

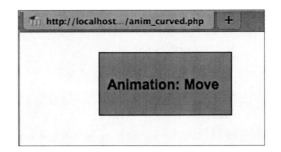

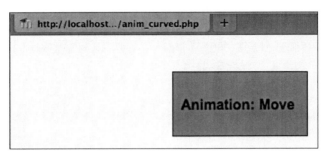

We begin by creating a PHP page to set up a basic Moodle programming environment. In this case, `anim_curved.php`, with the following content:

```php
<?php
require_once(dirname(__FILE__) . '/../config.php');

$PAGE->set_context(get_context_instance(CONTEXT_SYSTEM));
$PAGE->set_url('/cook/anim_curved.php');
$PAGE->requires->js('/cook/anim_curved.js', true);

echo $OUTPUT->header();
?>
<div id="anim-container" style="border:1px solid black;background-colo
r:#0099FF;padding:10px;width:150px;margin:30px;">

<h1>Animation: Move</h1>

</div>
<?php
echo $OUTPUT->footer();
?>
```

We also create an associated JavaScript file `anim_curved.js`, where we will add the animation code, with the following content:

```
YUI().use("anim", function(Y) {

var startX = Y.one('#anim-container').getX();
var startY = Y.one('#anim-container').getY();

var anim = new Y.Anim({
        node: '#anim-container',
        to: {
         curve:
         [
             [startX+40, startY-40],
             [startX+160, startY]
         ]
        }
});
    Y.on("contentready", function ()
    {
        anim.run();
    }, "#anim-container");

});
```

How it works...

We start with a simple `div` element that we will move along a curved path.

In our JavaScript file, we begin by creating a new `anim` object, base on our `div` by passing in the `div`'s ID.

Next, we subscribe to the `div`'s `contentready` function, and add our animation code. First, we retrieve the current X and Y coordinates of the object, so we can know the starting position for the animation.

Next, we use the `set` method to add a `to` property, which we will set to a "curve" object containing the array matrix of the X and Y coordinates that describe the curve we wish our object to follow.

When our `div` is loaded and our animation code is run, YUI animates the motion of our object by moving it to each of the X and Y coordinate pairs we specified in turn. This has the effect of moving our `div` along a path shape matching that which is described by the coordinates we specified.

Changing an element's color

In this recipe, we will animate an element changing color. We will change the background color of the div element from blue to green.

Here, we can see the key steps in this animation by looking at a selection of frames:

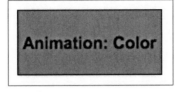

How to do it...

We begin by creating a PHP page to set up a basic Moodle programming environment. In this case, anim_color.php, with the following content:

```php
<?php
require_once(dirname(__FILE__) . '/../config.php');

$PAGE->set_context(get_context_instance(CONTEXT_SYSTEM));
$PAGE->set_url('/cook/anim_color.php');
$PAGE->requires->js('/cook/anim_color.js', true);

echo $OUTPUT->header();
?>
<div id="anim-container" style="border:1px solid black;background-colo
r:#0099FF;float:left;padding:5px;">

<h1>Animation: Color</h1>

</div>
```

```php
<?php
echo $OUTPUT->footer();

?>
```

We also create an associated JavaScript file, `anim_color.js`, where we will add the animation code, with the following content:

```javascript
YUI().use("node", "anim", function(Y) {

var anim = new Y.Anim({
        node: '#anim-container',
        to: {
         backgroundColor:'#2EC95D'
         }
});
    Y.on("contentready", function ()
    {
        anim.run();
    }, "#anim-container");

});
```

How it works...

We start with a simple `div` element with a specific background, in this case, blue.

Moving on to our JavaScript, we start by creating a new `anim` element based on our `div`, by specifying the `div`'s ID attribute as the node property. Additionally, we will set the `to` property, setting the `backgroundColor` attribute of the object to its new color, in this case green.

Finally, we set the animation to run once the `div` has loaded through the `contentready` event.

When the `div` element is loaded, its `contentready` event is fired and our animation is run. The element's color is changed from its initial blue state to the green we specified, over the default time span of 1 second.

Sequencing multiple animations

We can change as many attributes as we want during one animation, but to get multiple animations to occur linearly (one after the other) we must use a new approach. YUI allows for this by providing an `end` event which is fired when an animation is complete. In this way, we may chain as many animations as we wish, one after the other.

In this recipe, we will chain two animations, reducing the size of a `div` element, and then fading it out.

Here, we can see the key steps in this animation by looking at a selection of frames:

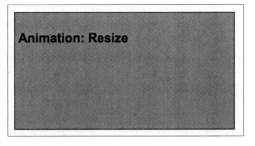

How to do it...

We begin by creating a PHP page to set up a basic Moodle programming environment. In this case, `anim_multiple.php`, with the following content:

```php
<?php
require_once(dirname(__FILE__) . '/../config.php');

$PAGE->set_context(get_context_instance(CONTEXT_SYSTEM));
$PAGE->set_url('/cook/anim_multiple');
$PAGE->requires->js('/cook/anim_multiple.js', true);

echo $OUTPUT->header();
?>
<div id="anim-container" style="border:1px solid black;background-color:#0099FF;float:left;padding:5px;width:300px;height:150px;opacity:1">

<h1>Animation: Resize</h1>

</div>
<?php
echo $OUTPUT->footer();

?>
```

We also create an associated JavaScript file, `anim_multiple.js`, where we will add the animation code, with the following content:

```javascript
YUI().use("node", "anim", function(Y) {
var anim = new Y.Anim({
        node: '#anim-container',
        to: {
         width:'180px',
         height:'50px'
         }
});

var animEnd = function()
{
   this.detach('end', animEnd);
   this.set('to', {opacity:0});
   this.run();
}
anim.on('end', animEnd);
   Y.on("contentready", function ()
   {
      anim.run();
   }, "#anim-container");

});
```

How it works...

We start with a `div` element that we will be animating, setting the desired height and width, and also setting a reference ID.

Next, we move on to the JavaScript code, beginning with creating a new `anim` object, passing the ID of our `div`. It is here that we will set up the first animation in the chain, namely, resizing the element by shrinking its width and height to 180px and 50px respectively.

Next, we will define the second animation in its own function, in this case, `animEnd`. This will later be attached to the first animation's `end` event. Because of this, the first step performed in this function will be to detach this event to ensure the second animation occurs only once. Next, we use the `set` method to fade-out the `div` by changing the opacity to 0. The final step to be performed inside this function is to set this animation to run itself.

Next, we register the function we just created `animEnd`, attaching it to the original `anim` object.

In the final step, we set the animation to run when the `div` has been loaded completely, through its `contentready` event.

The initial animation occurs in the standard fashion, animating the shrinking of the `div` element. As we have attached a function to the animation's `end` event, this is called next upon completion of the first "shrink" animation.

The second animation is then activated from this event, causing the element to fade-out to opacity 0, completing the chain of two animations.

Further animations may be sequenced by adding additional `end` event handlers in a sequence, that is, a third animation may be added by adding it to the animation's `end` event handler, from the second animation's `event` handler function, and so on.

9

Integrating External Libraries

In this chapter, we will cover:

- ▶ Adding the jQuery framework
- ▶ Adding the MooTools framework
- ▶ Adding the Dojo framework
- ▶ Adding the Prototype framework
- ▶ Adding the `script.aculo.us` add-on to Prototype
- ▶ Adding image enlargement with Lightbox 2

Introduction

In this chapter, we will look at the methods available to us for integrating external JavaScript libraries. The built-in JavaScript framework library, YUI, is powerful and feature-rich and can accomplish much, as we have seen in previous chapters. However, there are various reasons why we may need to make use of additional external libraries (for example, to implement something that is not possible with the YUI, or to make use of pre-written code that uses a specific framework).

Consider carefully whether or not you really need to add additional libraries, and weigh the benefits of the extra functionality that will be available against the extra complexity of adding and maintaining additional libraries.

We will look at how to set up some of the more commonly used frameworks, and implement a basic "content ready" event handler for each one, that is, setting up JavaScript code primed to run when a particular element is fully loaded by the browser. Finally, we will look at some extensions for the Prototype framework, namely the `script.aculo.us` add-on. We will finish by implementing the Lightbox image-viewer extension.

Adding the jQuery framework

The jQuery framework is a very well established framework, which is actively maintained and supported. It has similar goals to that of the YUI, namely to wrap up the most frequently used features of JavaScript, such as manipulating DOM elements, into a reusable, clean, cross-platform library. You may decide to use this framework in situations where you have a significant amount of pre-written code for the jQuery framework and it is not feasible for whatever reason to rewrite it as native JavaScript or YUI library code.

In this recipe, we will set up the jQuery framework, and write a small piece of code to verify that the library has loaded and is working correctly.

Getting ready

We begin by downloading the latest version of the jQuery framework. Visit the jQuery homepage at `http://jquery.com/`, and download the latest production version. Save this file to a location within your Moodle installation. In this example, we will save it in a directory named `cook` in the main Moodle site files directory.

 If you will be making use of any external framework, including jQuery, from more than one module, you may consider saving the framework files to a shared location, such as the `/lib` folder of your Moodle installation. This allows you to maintain one central copy of the framework, without the inconvenience of maintaining and updating multiple copies in different locations.

We now have a copy of the jQuery framework saved locally. We can create a page to initialize the framework and run some jQuery code to ensure that it is working correctly.

How to do it...

First, we create a new PHP page where we will setup a basic Moodle programming environment, and include the necessary files to run jQuery code. In this example, we create a file named `external_jquery.php` with the following content:

```php
<?php
require_once(dirname(__FILE__) . '/../config.php');
$PAGE->set_context(get_context_instance(CONTEXT_SYSTEM));
```

```
$PAGE->set_url('/cook/external_jquery.php');
$PAGE->requires->js('/cook/jquery-1.4.4.min.js');
$PAGE->requires->js('/cook/external_jquery.js');

echo $OUTPUT->header();

echo $OUTPUT->footer();

?>
```

Next, we create an associated JavaScript file into which we add the jQuery code as follows:

```
$(document).ready(function(){
   alert('Hello from jQuery');
});
```

Now when we run this page in a browser, we will see the following JavaScript alert pop-up appear, and we can be sure that jQuery has loaded correctly:

How it works...

After we have saved a copy of jQuery into our Moodle installation, we can create a PHP page in which to initialize the framework. We create this file and set up the Moodle programming environment, adding two JavaScript `includes`. The first file to include is the jQuery file, and the second is our custom JavaScript file which will contain our own code which makes use of the jQuery framework. Note that the main jQuery file must be included before any JavaScript that uses the framework.

Simply including the jQuery file: `$PAGE->requires->js('/cook/jquery-1.4.4.min.js');` in our page ensures that the framework is initialized and ready for use. In this example, we included a very simple use of the framework, namely using the `ready` event of the page's document object to display a JavaScript alert, confirming that the framework is working correctly.

Adding the MooTools framework

In this recipe, we will set up the MooTools framework for use in our example page.

The following is a quick overview of the framework from the MooTools website (http://mootools.net/):

> *MooTools is a compact, modular, Object-Oriented JavaScript framework designed for the intermediate to advanced JavaScript developer. It allows you to write powerful, flexible, and cross-browser code with its elegant, well documented, and coherent API.*

MooTools is essentially another alternative to YUI or jQuery. You may want to install this framework if you wish to make use of some third party code based on MooTools, which is either not possible or impractical to port to native JavaScript. You can also rewrite it using Moodle's preferred JavaScript framework, YUI.

We will create a simple MooTools script which will display a JavaScript alert when the domready event is fired.

Getting ready

We begin by downloading the latest version of the MooTools framework. Visit the MooTools homepage at http://mootools.net/, navigate to the download page, and download a suitable version of MooTools. In this example, we will use the compressed version of MooTools Core 1.3 without compatibility.

Save this file to a location within your Moodle installation. In this example, we will save it in a directory named cook in the main Moodle site files directory.

How to do it...

Setup a PHP page, external_mootools.php, that will be used to set up MooTools with the following content:

```php
<?php
require_once(dirname(__FILE__) . '/../config.php');
$PAGE->set_context(get_context_instance(CONTEXT_SYSTEM));
$PAGE->set_url('/cook/external_mootools.php');
$PAGE->requires->js('/cook/mootools-core-1.3.js');
$PAGE->requires->js('/cook/external_mootools.js');
echo $OUTPUT->header();
echo $OUTPUT->footer();
?>
```

Finally, we create a JavaScript file, external_mootools.js, into which we will add a simple MooTools script, as follows:

```
window.addEvent('domready', function() {
    alert('Hello from MooTools');
});
```

Once we have saved a copy of MooTools into our Moodle installation, we can set up a PHP file to create the page which will run the MooTools code. We include two JavaScript files, the first being the MooTools file, and the second being our custom JavaScript file `external_mootools.js`. Note that the MooTools file must be included before the file that makes use of it.

We can now load this page in a web browser, and we will see the following JavaScript alert pop-up, proving to us that MooTools has loaded correctly, ready for use:

How it works...

We loaded the MooTools framework before our own JavaScript file, ensuring the framework is ready for use. The JavaScript code we added here makes use of the window's `domready` event to display a JavaScript alert after the page has fully loaded. When we load the page, we see the alert pop-up, and can be assured that MooTools has loaded correctly.

Adding the Dojo framework

In this recipe, we will set up the Dojo framework for use within Moodle. We will then create a simple Dojo script which displays a JavaScript alert when the page has fully loaded, making use of Dojo's `addOnLoad` feature.

A brief description of the framework from the Dojo website (`http://dojotoolkit.org/`):

> *Dojo saves you time, delivers powerful performance, and scales with your development process. It's the toolkit experienced developers turn to for building superior desktop and mobile web experiences.*

A typical need for installing this framework would be a situation where you wish to make use of a third party code, which has been written on top of the Dojo framework and it is either not possible, or it is impractical, to re-implement it as either native JavaScript code, or based on top of Moodle's preferred JavaScript library, YUI.

Getting ready

First, we need to obtain a copy of the Dojo framework file. Visit the Dojo website at `http://dojotoolkit.org/`, and navigate to the download section. Download a copy of the compressed framework and save it to a location within your Moodle installation. In this example, we will save it to the `cook` directory along with our other files.

How to do it...

We can now move on to creating a page, `external_dojo.php`, where we will set up the Moodle programming environment, and include the Dojo file. Create a PHP file with the following content:

```php
<?php

require_once(dirname(__FILE__) . '/../config.php');

$PAGE->set_context(get_context_instance(CONTEXT_SYSTEM));
$PAGE->set_url('/cook/external_dojo.php');
$PAGE->requires->js('/cook/dojo.js');
$PAGE->requires->js('/cook/external_dojo.js');

echo $OUTPUT->header();

echo $OUTPUT->footer();

?>
```

Finally, we create a JavaScript file, `external_dojo.js`, into which we will add our Dojo code, as follows:

```javascript
dojo.addOnLoad(function()
{
    alert('Hello from dojo');
});
```

Once we have saved a local copy of the Dojo framework alongside our Moodle page, we can include it in the page, along with our own JavaScript file. We ensure that we load the Dojo framework before we load our own JavaScript file, which contains the code that makes use of the Dojo framework.

Finally, we can test the page in a browser, and see the following JavaScript alert is displayed, indicating that the dojo framework is fully loaded, ready for use:

How it works...

The PHP loads as normal, and includes our local copy of the Dojo framework within the page. Next, our JavaScript file is included, which uses Dojo to register some JavaScript to run when the page has fully loaded, through the addOnLoad method. When the page has been loaded completely, the load event is fired and our script is executed. In this case, our script is displaying a JavaScript alert. When we see this occur, we can be assured that the Dojo framework has loaded correctly.

Adding the Prototype framework

In this recipe, we will set up the Prototype framework for use in our Moodle page. We will then set up a simple Prototype script to display a JavaScript alert when this page has been loaded completely.

The following is a brief description of the framework from the Prototype website (http://www.prototypejs.org/):

> *Prototype is a JavaScript Framework that aims to ease development of dynamic web applications.*
>
> *Featuring a unique, easy-to-use toolkit for class-driven development and the nicest Ajax library around, Prototype is quickly becoming the codebase of choice for web application developers everywhere.*

Prototype is the basis for two extensions: script.aculo.us and Lightbox. We will look at these in the next two recipes to further enhance the features available to us.

Getting ready

We begin by obtaining a copy of the Prototype framework. Visit the Prototype website at http://www.prototypejs.org/, and navigate to the download section. Download the latest stable version, and save it to our cook directory along with the other files used in this recipe.

How to do it...

We now have a local copy of Prototype available. We can create a page, `external_prototype.php`, where we will load the framework along with our own custom JavaScript file, as follows:

```php
<?php
require_once(dirname(__FILE__) . '/../config.php');
$PAGE->set_context(get_context_instance(CONTEXT_SYSTEM));
$PAGE->set_url('/cook/external_prototype.php');
$PAGE->requires->js('/cook/prototype.js');
$PAGE->requires->js('/cook/external_prototype.js');
echo $OUTPUT->header();
echo $OUTPUT->footer();
?>
```

Finally, we create our custom JavaScript file, `external_prototype.js`, with the following content:

```javascript
document.observe("dom:loaded", function() {
    alert('Hello from Prototype');
});
```

We create a PHP file which sets up the Moodle programming environment, and load the Prototype framework file. Once the Prototype file has been loaded, we can add our own custom JavaScript file containing the script that makes use of Prototype. In this script, we use the `document.observe` method of Prototype to attach a JavaScript alert to the page's `load` event.

When we load this page in a browser, we see that this event has been fired, and the JavaScript alert is displayed, as shown in the following screenshot:

The page at http://localhost says:

Hello from Prototype

OK

How it works...

The PHP file loads the Prototype framework first. This ensures that it has been loaded and is ready for use before our custom JavaScript that uses the framework is loaded. Next, our JavaScript is loaded, and uses Prototype to register a JavaScript alert to run when the page has finished loading. When the page is completely loaded in the browser, we will see the JavaScript alert pop-up, confirming that the Prototype framework has loaded correctly.

Adding the script.aculo.us add-on to Prototype

The `script.aculo.us` library is an add-on for Prototype that contains several user interface enhancements such as animation, drag-and-drop and AJAX controls. In this recipe, we will set up `script.aculo.us` and add a `shake` animation effect to verify it has loaded correctly.

Getting ready

First, we need to obtain a copy of `script.aculo.us` by visiting `http://script.aculo.us/`, and navigating to the download page. Download the ZIP archive of the current version, and unzip it into a folder named `scriptaculous` inside the `cook` subdirectory of the Moodle installation used in this example, that is, `/path/to/moodle/cook/scriptaculous`.

How to do it...

Create a PHP file, `external_scriptaculous.php`, with the following content:

```php
<?php
require_once(dirname(__FILE__) . '/../config.php');

$PAGE->set_context(get_context_instance(CONTEXT_SYSTEM));
$PAGE->set_url('/cook/external_scriptaculous.php');
$PAGE->requires->js('/cook/prototype.js');
$PAGE->requires->js('/cook/scriptaculous/scriptaculous.js');
$PAGE->requires->js('/cook/scriptaculous/effects.js');
$PAGE->requires->js('/cook/external_scriptaculous.js');

echo $OUTPUT->header();

?>
<div id="demo">Hello from script.aculo.us</div>
<?php

echo $OUTPUT->footer();

?>
```

Finally, we create a JavaScript file, `external_scriptaculous.js`, with the following content:

```javascript
document.observe("dom:loaded", function()
{
    Effect.Shake('demo');
});
```

Now when we load this page in a web browser, we can see the shake effect in action. The following screenshots show a selection of frames from the shake effect animation. Note that the text to which we have applied the effect is shifted back and forth from left to right, as if the text is being shaken from side to side, before settling back to its original position:

How it works...

First, we download the `script.aculo.us` files and save them in a folder named `scriptaculous` alongside our Moodle files in the `cook` subdirectory.

Next, we create a PHP file where we will load the necessary JavaScript files. They are, in order:

1. `/cook/prototype.js`
2. `/cook/scriptaculous/scriptaculous.js`
3. `/cook/scriptaculous/effects.js`
4. `/cook/external_scriptaculous.js`

We now add a `div` tag to the body of the PHP page, which contains some sample text. We will apply the shake animation effect to this element, so we add an ID to the tag for future reference.

Finally, we add some code to our JavaScript file `external_scriptaculous.js`. We set up a page load function, using Prototype as in the previous recipe. Inside this function, we will use `script.aculo.us` to apply a shake animation effect to our `div` element.

When we load the PHP page in our browser, the PHP code loads all of the required JavaScript files in the specified order. This order ensures that the dependency hierarchy is correct, meaning that Prototype is loaded before the `script.aculo.us` add-ons, and finally our custom JavaScript that makes use of the `script.aculo.us` add-on gets loaded.

When our custom script file, `external_scriptaculous.js`, is loaded, it registers the shake animation on our `div` element to fire when the page is loaded completely. Finally, when the entire page has loaded completely in the browser, the load event is fired and we see the shake animation applied to our `div` tag.

Adding image enlargement with Lightbox 2

Lightbox 2 is a very popular script based on `script.aculo.us` (and in turn, based on Prototype) which provides a slick way to open links to high-resolution versions of thumbnail images in a modal window.

In this recipe, we will integrate Lightbox 2 into our page, and add an image thumbnail to which we will apply the Lightbox 2 functionality.

Getting ready

First, we need to obtain a copy of Lightbox 2, by visiting `http://www.huddletogether.com/projects/lightbox2/`, and navigating to the download section. Download the ZIP file of the latest version, and unpack it to the `cook` subdirectory of the Moodle installation used in this example, that is, `/path/to/moodle/cook/lightbox2`.

 Lightbox 2 contains links to images that are relative to the page on which you have loaded the script. To ensure that these images are available to the script, copy the images folder to the same location as your script, in our example, `/path/to/moodle/cook/images`.

How to do it...

Create a PHP page, `external_lightbox.php`, in which to set up Lightbox 2. Note that we will require a sample image for the example, in this case `flower.jpg`:

The content of the PHP file is as follows:

```php
<?php
require_once(dirname(__FILE__) . '/../config.php');

$PAGE->set_context(get_context_instance(CONTEXT_SYSTEM));
$PAGE->set_url('/cook/external_lightbox.php');

$PAGE->requires->js('/cook/prototype.js');
$PAGE->requires->js('/cook/scriptaculous/scriptaculous.js');
$PAGE->requires->js('/cook/scriptaculous/effects.js');
$PAGE->requires->js('/cook/scriptaculous/builder.js');
$PAGE->requires->js('/cook/lightbox2/js/lightbox.js');

$PAGE->requires->css('/cook/lightbox2/css/lightbox.css');

echo $OUTPUT->header();

?>
<a href="flower.jpg" rel="lightbox"><img src="flower.jpg" width="150"
/></a>
<?php

echo $OUTPUT->footer();

?>
```

We can now load this page in a web browser, and see the enhanced Lightbox image viewer in action. Firstly, a thumbnail of the flower image is displayed as normal:

We can now click on this thumbnail to activate the detailed view of the full resolution image inside the modal Lightbox window, as shown in the following screenshot:

How it works...

Once we have downloaded Lightbox 2 and saved it to a suitable location, we can begin implementing it in our PHP page `external_lightbox.php`. After setting up the standard Moodle programming environment, we begin including the following necessary JavaScript files, in specific order:

1. `/cook/prototype.js`
2. `/cook/scriptaculous/scriptaculous.js`
3. `/cook/scriptaculous/effects.js`
4. `/cook/scriptaculous/builder.js`
5. `/cook/lightbox2/js/lightbox.js`

The order is important, as there is a hierarchy of dependence. This means Lightbox 2 requires `script.aculo.us` to be available, and in turn, `script.aculo.us` requires Prototype to be available.

Next, we include the Lightbox 2 CSS file `/cook/lightbox2/css/lightbox.css`.

Finally, we add a thumbnail of our sample image, `flower.jpg`, and enclose it in a link (`<a>` tag) to the high-resolution version. We activate Lightbox 2 functionality on this thumbnail by adding a `rel` attribute and setting its value to `lightbox`. Now when we load the page, and click on the link, we see that the high-resolution image is displayed in an attractive modal image viewer.

There's more...

Lightbox 2 is very unobtrusive, which uses progressive enhancement techniques. This means we need to make only minimal changes to our existing HTML markup, that is, simply add the required `rel` attribute to the images for which we wish to enable Lightbox. The result of this is that if JavaScript is not available in the user's browser, they will still have a regular link through the high-resolution version of the image.

Once all the requisite JavaScript and CSS files are loaded correctly in the page, Lightbox 2 will seamlessly activate the modal image viewer for all hyperlinks with the `rel="lightbox"` attribute set.

Index

D

data
  displaying 83, 85
  loading, from external domain
    using PHP 63, 64
  retrieving, from Moodle 2.0 wed
    service 72-76
data.csv file 70
data.json file 67
data paging, data tables
  enabling 87
DataSource
  using, for parsing CSV data 69-72
  using, for parsing JSON 67-69
  using, for parsing XML 64-66
datasource_csv.js file 70
datasource_csv.php file 70
datasource_json.js file 68
datasource_json.php file 67
DataSourceJSONSchema plugin 69
datasource_moodlews.js file 73
datasource_moodlews.php file 72
DataSource object 83
DataSourceTextSchema plugin 71
datasource_xml.js 65
datasource_xml.php file 64
DataSourceXMLSchema plugin 66, 75
DataTable constructor 85
data tables
  basic column sorting 85, 86
  data paging 87
  editing, enabling 89-91
  in-line editing 80
  paging 80
  scrolling 80
  scrolling, enabling 88
  sorting 79
  working with 79
data.xml file 64
dirname function 11
div element 95, 133
Dojo framework
  about 151
  downloading 152
  setting up 151, 152
  URL 151

working 153
domready event 30
drop-down navigation menu
  about 109
  adding 109

E

easing behaviors
  URL 134
editing, data tables
  enabling 89-91
editor property 91
element
  color, changing 141, 142
  fade-in effect, producing 124-126
  fade-out effect, producing 126-128
  moving, along curved path 138-140
  moving, along straight path 136-138
  resizing 132, 133
  scrolling 129-131
email validation type 46
end event 142
event-delegate module 35
event delegation
  about 34
  implementing 33-35
event handler function 145
Extension and Application Repository (PEAR)
  library 40
external URIs
  requesting, using IO's alternative transport
    method 60, 62

F

fade-in effect
  producing 124-126
fade-out effect
  producing 126-128
failed event 63
failure callback function 66
fly-out navigation menu
  about 106
  fadding 106-112
form validation 40
Function data source 99

Thank you for buying
Moodle JavaScript Cookbook

About Packt Publishing

Packt, pronounced 'packed', published its first book "*Mastering phpMyAdmin for Effective MySQL Management*" in April 2004 and subsequently continued to specialize in publishing highly focused books on specific technologies and solutions.

Our books and publications share the experiences of your fellow IT professionals in adapting and customizing today's systems, applications, and frameworks. Our solution based books give you the knowledge and power to customize the software and technologies you're using to get the job done. Packt books are more specific and less general than the IT books you have seen in the past. Our unique business model allows us to bring you more focused information, giving you more of what you need to know, and less of what you don't.

Packt is a modern, yet unique publishing company, which focuses on producing quality, cutting-edge books for communities of developers, administrators, and newbies alike. For more information, please visit our website: www.packtpub.com.

About Packt Open Source

In 2010, Packt launched two new brands, Packt Open Source and Packt Enterprise, in order to continue its focus on specialization. This book is part of the Packt Open Source brand, home to books published on software built around Open Source licences, and offering information to anybody from advanced developers to budding web designers. The Open Source brand also runs Packt's Open Source Royalty Scheme, by which Packt gives a royalty to each Open Source project about whose software a book is sold.

Writing for Packt

We welcome all inquiries from people who are interested in authoring. Book proposals should be sent to author@packtpub.com. If your book idea is still at an early stage and you would like to discuss it first before writing a formal book proposal, contact us; one of our commissioning editors will get in touch with you.

We're not just looking for published authors; if you have strong technical skills but no writing experience, our experienced editors can help you develop a writing career, or simply get some additional reward for your expertise.

Lightning Source UK Ltd.
Milton Keynes UK
UKOW012243010812

196907UK00003BA/49/P